Cast Iron Skillet Cookbook Box Set

Delicious Breakfast, Lunch, Dinner, Dessert And Side Dish Recipes In A Cast Iron Skillet

(4 Books In 1)

TERESA SLOAT

Copyright © 2015 Teresa Sloat

All rights reserved. No part of this publication may be reproduced, distributed, or transmitted in any form or by any means, including photocopying, recording, or other electronic or mechanical methods, without the prior written permission of the publisher, except in the case of brief quotations embodied in critical reviews and certain other noncommercial uses permitted by copyright law.

ISBN-13: 978-1514827147

ISBN-10: 151482714X

DEDICATION

To all owners of cast iron skillet and those who love delicious meals.

TABLE OF CONTENTS

BOOK 1 1

CAST IRON SKILLET COOKBOOK: VOL.1 BREAKFAST RECIPES.................... 1

Introduction 1

CAST IRON SKILLET BREAKFAST RECIPES 4

    Zucchini Egg Skillet 4

    Cast Iron Skillet Feta Frittata 5

    Herbed Tart 6

    Spicy Egg Scramble 7

    French Bread Pizza 8

    Mexican Breakfast Lasagna 9

    Caramelized Bacon Twists 10

    Cast Iron Skillet Gravy 11

    Breakfast Pizza With Tater Tots 11

    Cast Iron Skillet Fried Potatoes & Eggs 13

    Sausage Egg Roll Ups 14

    Breakfast Mac & Cheese 15

    Breakfast Enchiladas 16

    Skillet Breakfast Relish 17

    Tasty Potato, Pepper & Egg Breakfast 19

    Cast Iron Skillet Strata 20

    Yummy Egg, Potato & Sausage 21

    Cast Iron Skillet Hash 22

    Cast Iron Skillet Shepherd's Breakfast 23

    Skillet Ham And Cheese Quiche 24

    Cast Iron Skillet Hash Brown Quiche 25

Spicy Breakfast Eggs 26

Breakfast Sweet Potato, Bacon & Egg 27

Woven Bacon Skillet 28

Baked Ham & Cheese Omelet 29

Cast Iron Skillet Bacon Cheese Biscuits 30

Bacon Spinach Breakfast Casserole 30

Loaded Baked Potato Breakfast Skillet 32

Seasoned Sausage, Egg & Cheese Breakfast Bread 33

Cast Iron Skillet Biscuits &Sausage Gravy 34

Sausage And Crescent Roll Bake 35

Ham And Sausage Hash Brown Egg Bake 36

Gingerbread French Toast Breakfast Bake 37

Cast Iron Skillet Apple Pancakes 38

Cast Iron Skillet French Toast 39

Butter Buttermilk Biscuits 40

Lemon Blueberry Scones 41

Cinnamon Rolls Skillet 42

Sugared Cinnamon Pecan Rolls 43

Light Blueberry Biscuits 44

Twin Berry Puff Pancakes 45

Cast Iron Maple Bacon French Toast 46

Cast Iron Skillet Coffee Cake 48

Apple Pie Breakfast Bake 49

Turtle Cinnamon Rolls 50

Cast Iron Skillet Cheese Danish 51

Fruit And Oatmeal Bake 52

Pancake And Sausage Casserole 53

Easy Cast Iron Doughnuts 54

Easy Glazed Doughnut Holes 55

Cast Iron Apple Fritters 56

Cast Iron Jelly Doughnuts 57

Popover Pancake 58

Cornmeal Pancake With Sausage & Maple Syrup 59

Potatoes, Bacon And Cheese 60

BOOK 2 62

CAST IRON SKILLET COOKBOOK: VOL.2 LUNCH RECIPES 62

Introduction 62

CAST IRON SKILLET LUNCH RECIPES 65

Tasty Buffalo Chicken Quesadillas 65

Buttermilk Chicken Tender 66

Cast Iron Skillet Chicken Ranch Pockets 66

Cast Iron Skillet Chicken Avocado Burritos 67

Cheddar Ranch Chicken Burgers 68

Coconut Chicken Skillet 69

Cast Iron Skillet Blackened Chicken Fajitas 70

Cast Iron Skillet Baked Chicken Breasts 71

Gnocchi Chicken Skillet 72

Skillet Chicken & Red Potatoes 73

Easy College Chicken Lunch 74

Baked 'N' Fried Chicken 75

Bacon, Turkey And Avocado Sandwich 76

Cast Iron Skillet Steak Sandwich 77

Flank Steak Sauté 78

Burger Ultimate 79

Hamburger Gravy Over Toasted Bread 80

Cast Iron Skillet Thai Basil Beef 81

Cast Iron Skillet Beef & Bean Burrito 82

Beef & Broccoli Skillet 83

Cast Iron Skillet Taco Pizza Rolls 84

Easy Baked French Dipped Sandwiches 85

Cast Iron Skillet Pork Burger 86

Skillet Boneless Pork Chops 87

Pineapple Teriyaki Pork Chops 88

Cast Iron Skillet Roasted Pork Medallions 89

Lemon Rosemary Pork Chops 90

Bruschetta Pork Chops 91

Cast Iron Skillet Pork & Ramen Stir-Fry 92

Honey And Soy Pork Chops 93

Hot Ham And Cheese 94

Cast Iron Shrimp Scampi Quesadillas 95

Skillet Salmon Croquette Balls With Dill Sauce 96

Tuna Quesadillas 97

Cast Iron Skillet Salmon Burger 98

Drained Tuna Melt 99

Cast Iron Skillet Fish Tacos 100

Cast Iron Skillet Fish And Chips 101

Beer Battered Fish And Potato Wedges 102

Cast Iron Skillet Fried Clams 103

Pan Seared Scallops 104

Beef Hot Dog Stir Fry 105

Cast Iron Skillet Kielbasa..106

Italian Grilled Cheese 107

Skillet Hawaiian Grilled Cheese 108

Cast Iron Skillet Barbecued Grilled Cheese 109

Clubhouse Grill In Skillet..109

Cast Iron Skillet Grilled Cheese 110

Cast Iron Skillet Pepperoni Pizza 111

Feta Flatbread Savor 112

Prosciutto Pizza With Mushroom & Leek 113

Vegetable Pizza 114

Cast Iron Skillet Nachos 115

Bacon Spicy Cheese Fries..116

Cast Iron Skillet Fried Eggplant 117

BOOK 3 119

CAST IRON SKILLET COOKBOOK: VOL.3 Dinner RECIPES 119

Introduction..119

CAST IRON SKILLET DINNER RECIPES 122

Cast Iron Skillet Chicken Casserole 122

Chicken Almondine 123

Stir-Fry Chicken..124

Cast Iron Skillet Chicken Alfredo..125

Cast Iron Skillet Lemon Garlic Chicken Pasta.......................................126

Cast Iron Skillet Chicken Drumsticks & Potatoes 127

Catalina Chicken...128

Swiss Chicken Casserole 128

Apricot Glazed Walnut Stuffed Chicken Breast With Potatoes 129

Cast Iron Skillet Chicken Cordon Bleu 131

Bourbon Spiced Chicken Wings 132

Pecan Crusted Chicken 133

Cast Iron Skillet Southwestern Fiesta Rice 135

Cast Iron Skillet Peanut Fried Chicken 136

Cast Iron Skillet Whole Roasted Chicken 137

Pan Roasted Chicken With Bacon & Apples 138

Skillet Chicken Parmesan 139

Cast Iron Skillet Chicken & Zucchini 140

Baked Ham 141

Cast Iron Skillet Pork Chop Dinner 142

Cast Iron Skillet Southern Fried Chicken 143

Cast Iron Skillet Pork Chops &Mushroom Gravy 144

Pork Chops With Thyme & Pineapple 145

Cast Iron Skillet Tuscan Pork Chops 146

Cast Iron Skillet Oven Baked Pork Chops 147

Island Pork Tenderloin 148

Cast Iron Skillet French Onion Pork Chops 149

Pork Chops With Brussels Sprouts And Sweet Potatoes 150

Cajun Spiced Pork Chops 151

Cast Iron Skillet Pork Chop Casserole 152

Baked Pork Chops On Rice 153

Cast Iron Skillet Pork Steaks 154

Pork Roast 155

Pork Chops With Scalloped Potatoes 156

Cast Iron Skillet Swedish Meatballs 157

Pepper Steak With Rice 158

Stuffed Cabbage Rolls 159

Cast Iron Skillet Hamburger Goulash 160

Cast Iron Skillet Sloppy Joes 161

Cast Iron Skillet Steak Meal 162

Cast Iron Skillet Meat Loaf 163

Cast Iron Skillet Stroganoff 164

Cast Iron Skillet Beef Tenderloin 164

Cast Iron Skillet Oven Stew 165

Cast Iron Skillet Salmon Loaf 166

Garlic Shrimp 167

Cast Iron Skillet Fried Cat Fish 168

Cast Iron Skillet Flounder 169

Salmon Patties 170

Crab Roll-ups 171

Polish Sausage And Sauerkraut 172

Corn Casserole With Smoked Sausage 173

Potato and Smoked Sausage Skillet 174

Lamb Chops 175

Venison Chops 175

BOOK 4 177

CAST IRON SKILLET COOKBOOK: VOL.4 DESSERT AND SIDE DISH RECIPES 177

Introduction 177

DESSERTS & SIDE DISHES 180

Broccoli Casserole	180
Cowboy Beans	181
Fried Cabbage	182
Cheesy Scalloped Potatoes	182
Potato Cakes	183
Fried Green Tomatoes	184
Baked Macaroni And Cheese	185
Corn Pudding	186
Scalloped Green Peppers	187
Green Bean Casserole	188
Rice Casserole	189
Maple-Glazed Carrots	189
Cast Iron Skillet Mexican Cornbread	190
Fried Okra	191
Roasted Vegetables	192
Caramelized Brussels Sprouts	193
Fried Squash Patties	194
Asparagus And Onions	194
Cornbread Stuffing	195
Onion Rings	196
Onion Pie	197
Creamed Spinach	198
Fried Corn	199
Fried Squash	200
Cast Iron Skillet Cauliflower	201
Cast Iron Skillet Asparagus	202

Cast Iron Skillet Carrot Cake 202

Caramel Nut Pound Cake 204

Heath Bar Cake 205

Cast Iron Skillet Honey Bun Cake 206

Fudge Cake 207

Crumb Cake 208

Brownie Pudding Cake 209

Chocolate Cobbler Cake 210

Blackberry Betty 211

Apple Pie 211

Cast Iron Skillet Pecan Pie 213

Lazy Fruit Cobbler 214

Cast Iron Skillet Peanut Butter Cookie 215

Cast Iron Skillet Blondies 216

Magic Cookie Bars 216

Oatmeal Cookie Patties 217

No-Crust Coconut Pie 219

Blueberry Bread 220

Cast Iron Skillet Strawberry Peach Tart 221

Cast Iron Skillet Berry Dessert 222

Cast Iron Skillet Monkey Bread 223

Cast Iron Skillet Strawberry Shortcake 224

Salted Caramel Apple Crumble 225

Cast Iron Skillet Smores 226

Blueberry & Cream Cheese Croissant Pudding 227

Banana Nut Bread 227

English Toffee 229

Cast Iron Skillet Crepes 229

Cast Iron Skillet Giant Chocolate Chip Cookie 230

BOOK 1

CAST IRON SKILLET COOKBOOK: VOL.1 BREAKFAST RECIPES

Introduction

The cast iron skillet has been handed down for generations. Many wonderful dishes have been created in the cast iron skillet. Most of us grew up with meals cooked in an iron skillet. There were not a lot of choices, stainless steel and coated skillets came along at a later date to make cooking seem easier. Dining out was a special occasion, home cooked meals were what we had. Fast food was not the choice of a meal. When at Grandma's, this was the essential cooking tool she used. Everything tasted better. Most people use it for cornbread or some meats, but the amazing creations are only beginning. Take a moment and think of recipes that can be whipped up in this great creation.

Cast iron skillets are durable and flexible. Simple dishes can be cooked or exotic cuisines can be created. They are not limited to the classic dishes. The cast iron skillet can be bought new or you can look at thrift stores, the older cast iron seems to be better made and sometimes lighter. They look old and rusty. Just a little preparation to get the skillet ready is all that is needed.

The first thing to do with the skillet is to season it. Cooking breakfast bacon can help that or oil the skillet all over, inside and out. Set your oven to 350F and place the skillet in the oven. Let it bake for about an hour. This should set the oil in your skillet. To clean the skillet, just wipe out or use plain water with a scrub brush to clean it. Do not use soapy water, it removes the seasoning from the skillet and can cause rust to build up. Always dry your skillet thoroughly after washing it. If rust does build up, you can clean the rust spots, re-oil them and heat in the oven again. They are very versatile and last a long, long time. Store your skillet with your normal cookware.

There is something about the taste of food cooked in a cast iron skillet. Your pan becomes seasoned over the years which in turn make your food more delectable. Meals from breakfast to dinner can be cooked in your skillet. Many desserts can be created. This versatile skillet can be used on top of the stove, in the oven or even on a campfire. Pack it up and take it with you on your family camping trips. Think of all the recipes you can make. Cleaning a cast iron skillet can be easy when camping. Use salt to scrub the debris out and re-oil and set aside until the next use.

Cast iron has great heat retention and distribution, which will cook your recipes more evenly. Did you know cooking in cast iron gives you extra needed iron in your body? Iron boosts your immune system. Great, isn't it? Toxic fumes can be avoided, just switch from non-stick to cast iron. The prices of cast iron are cheaper than other types of cookware. The biggest problem is food sticking. If the skillet is seasoned, oiled and maintained well, this should be simple to alleviate.

Meats are a wonderful item to cook in a cast iron skillet. Searing and stir-fries are meant for these skillets. Vegetables and eggs cook up nicely. Frying is the number one job for a cast iron skillet. Normally we think of fried chicken, but all other meats turn out great also.

Admit it; we are all timid when it comes to cooking in cast iron. We store them away and out of sight. There is no need to be scared, just start experimenting with your skillet and your recipes. The more you cook in it, the more comfortable you become with using it.

It may be a good idea to have 2 skillets. One skillet is seasoned great for meats and vegetables. However, you do not want your desserts to taste like steak or chicken. Invest in a second skillet for desserts, cornbread and biscuits. This will result in tasty and delectable desserts.

Needless to say, cooking in a cast iron skillet can range from searing, braising, baking and frying. Any dish you attempt will taste wonderful and will be asked for again and again. Breakfast recipes are the best to start with. Take a weekend and indulge your family with eggs, bacon or sausage, biscuits or hashbrowns. Throw in a few other vegetables and other seasoning and you have a delicious meal. All you need are volunteers to eat them, which I'm sure will be no problem to find.

Get out the iron skillet, brush off the dust, oil and season it. Take a moment to decide what great breakfast dish you want to cook for your family and begin preparing your meal. Dare to be different!

CAST IRON SKILLET BREAKFAST RECIPES

Zucchini Egg Skillet
Serves: 4

Cooking Time: 30 minutes

Ingredients:

Olive Oil, 2 Tbsp

Red Potatoes, 2 medium, cubed

Onion, 1 medium, chopped

Zucchini, 2 small, shredded

Sweet red peppers, ½, cleaned and chopped

Cherry Tomatoes, 6 quartered

Salt, ¼ tsp

Pepper, ¼ tsp

Cheddar Cheese, ½ cup

Eggs, 4

Directions:

1. Heat oil in cast iron skillet. Cook potatoes and onions for 6 minutes.

2. Add in zucchini. Cook for 5 more minutes.

3. Stir in peppers, cherry tomatoes, salt and pepper.

4. Sprinkle with cheese.

5. Break eggs on top.

6. Cook for 20 minutes or until eggs are done.

7. Serve warm.

8. Breakfast meat can be added.

Cast Iron Skillet Feta Frittata

Serves: 2

Cooking Time: 20 minutes

Ingredients:

Olive Oil, 2 Tbsp

Green Onion, 1 chopped

Garlic clove, 1 minced

Eggs, 2

Egg substitute, ½ cup

Feta Cheese, 4 Tbsp

Tomatoes, ⅓ cup chopped

Avocado, 4 slices peeled

Sour Cream, 2 Tbsp

Directions:

1. Heat oil in cast iron skillet. Cook onions and garlic slightly.

2. Combine eggs, egg substitute and 3 Tbsp. of cheese.

3. Cook for 5 minutes.

4. Spread tomatoes and remaining cheese, cover and cook for 5 minutes.

5. Cook for 5 to 10 minutes more until egg mixture is set.

6. Slice and serve with avocado and sour cream.

Herbed Tart

Serves: 4

Cooking Time: 20 minutes

Ingredients:

Bacon strips, 4

Mushrooms, 1 cup sliced

Green Onions, 2 Tbsp

Olive Oil, 1 Tbsp

Tarragon, 1 tsp

Swiss cheese, ¼ cup shredded

Sour Cream, 3 Tbsp

Pepper, ¼ tsp

Puff Pastry, 1 sheet, thawed

Eggs, 5

Water, 1 tsp

Chives, 1 Tbsp

Salt, ¼ tsp

Directions:

1. In cast iron skillet, cook bacon, remove and drain.

2. Sauté the mushrooms and onions in olive oil, add tarragon.

3. Remove and stir in cheese, sour cream, salt and pepper.

4. Remove puff pastry and spread in cast iron skillet and prick.

5. Spread mushrooms and onion mix on pastry.

6. Place bacon on top.

7. Mix egg and water. Brush on edges of puff pastry.

8. Bake for 10 minutes.

9. Break remaining 4 eggs in each corner. Bake 10 more minutes.

10. Spread chives, salt and pepper.

11. Cut into 4 slices and serve.

Spicy Egg Scramble
Serves: 6

Cooking Time: 20 minutes

Ingredients:

Cooking Spray

Onion, ½ cup chopped

Green Pepper, ¼ cup chopped

Jalapeno Pepper, 1 seeded and chopped

Bacon, 8 slices, cooked and crumbled

Eggs, 8 beaten

Cheddar Cheese, 1 cup, shredded

Salt, ½ cup

Pepper, ¼ cup

Salsa, 1 cup

Directions:

1. Coat cast iron skillet with cooking spray.

2. Sauté onions and peppers until tender.

3. Add bacon; pour eggs over bacon, onions and peppers.

4. Sprinkle with cheese, salt and pepper.

5. Cook for about 30 minutes until eggs are set. Stir constantly.

6. Serve with salsa and toast.

French Bread Pizza

Serves: 4

Cooking Time: 20 minutes

Ingredients:

French bread, 1 slice

Alfredo Sauce, 1 ⅓ cups

Italian Sausage, links, chopped

Olives, 1 can, sliced and drained

Onion, 1 small, chopped

Broccoli, ½ cup, chopped

Cauliflower, ½ cup, chopped

Mushrooms, 1 ¼ cups, sliced

Mozzarella Cheese, 1 ½ cup, shredded

Directions:

1. Slice French bread in 2 slices long ways.

2. Place in cast iron skillet and spread Alfredo sauce over each half.

3. Spread, sausage, olives, onion, broccoli, cauliflower and mushrooms on each half of bread.

4. Sprinkle cheese over bread.

5. Bake in 350F preheated oven for 20 minutes.

6. Remove and serve.

Mexican Breakfast Lasagna

Serves: 4

Cooking Time: 20 minutes

Ingredients:

Oil, 1 Tbsp

Cherry Tomatoes, 10 oz., chopped

Cilantro, 2 Tbsp

Jalapeno pepper, 1 med. chopped

Onion, 2 tsp

Lime Juice, 1 Tbsp.

Salt, ¼ tsp

Pepper, ¼ tsp

Eggs, 12, scrambled

Butter, 1 Tbsp

Flour Tortillas, 12

Cheddar Cheese, 10 oz., grated

Corn Salsa, 1 jar

Directions:

1. Heat oil in skillet, whisk eggs, salt and pepper together and scramble lightly.

2. Mix tomatoes, cilantro, jalapeno and onion. Add lime juice, salt and pepper.

3. Butter cast iron skillet. Line skillet with tortillas.

4. Spread egg mixture over tortillas, sprinkle with cheese, and top with corn salsa. Sprinkle with more cheese.

5. Repeat layers.

6. Bake in 350F preheated oven for 20 minutes.

7. Remove, allow to set, then slice and serve.

Caramelized Bacon Twists
Serves: 9

Cooking Time: 25 minutes

Ingredients:

Bacon, 1 lb

Brown Sugar, ½ cup

Cinnamon, 2 tsp

Directions:

1. Mix brown sugar and cinnamon together.

2. Cut bacon in half; dip in sugar and cinnamon and twist.

3. Place in foil lined cast iron skillet.

4. Bake in 350F preheated oven for 25 minutes.

5. Serve warm or cool.

Cast Iron Skillet Gravy
Serves: 4

Cooking Time: 25 to 30 minutes

Ingredients:

Sausage drippings, 2 Tbsp

Flour, 2 Tbsp

Milk, 2 cups

Salt, 1 tsp

Pepper, 1 tsp

Directions:

1. Heat sausage drippings in cast iron skillet.

2. Add flour, salt and pepper. Stir and brown lightly. It will be lumpy.

3. Add milk and continue stirring over medium heat for 30 minutes or until gravy is smooth and thickened.

4. You can serve over biscuits baked in a cast iron skillet.

Breakfast Pizza With Tater Tots
Serves: 6

Cooking Time: 20 to 25 minutes

Ingredients:

Pizza dough, 1 lb

Olive Oil, 2 Tbsp

Provolone Cheese, 5 slices

Tater tots, 1 cup, baked

Bacon, 4 thick slices, cooked and chopped

Canadian bacon, 3 slices, chopped

Eggs, 3 large

Salt, ¼ tsp

Pepper, ¼ tsp

Chives, 1 tsp

Thyme, 1 tsp

Directions:

1. Oil cast iron skillet and spread pizza dough in it.

2. Coat top of dough with olive oil.

3. Place cheese over dough. Add bacon and Canadian bacon.

4. Spread tater tots on top of bacon. Add thyme and chives.

5. Heat on stove for 5 minutes.

6. Remove and crack eggs on top of bacon and tater tots.

7. Bake in 450F preheated oven for 20 to 25 minutes until eggs are set.

8. Remove and slice.

9. Serve warm.

Cast Iron Skillet Fried Potatoes & Eggs

Serves: 4

Cooking Time: 30 minutes

Ingredients:

Oil, 2 Tbsp

Potatoes, 3, washed and sliced

Onions, 1 sliced

Salt, ¼ tsp

Garlic Powder, 1 tsp

Seasoning Salt, 1 tsp

Rosemary, 1 tsp

Thyme, 1 tsp

Pepper, 1 tsp

Eggs, 4

Directions:

1. Heat oil in cast iron skillet over medium heat.

2. Add sliced potatoes, onions and spices.

3. Cook for 20 minutes covered until potatoes are tender, stirring occasionally. Uncover and crack eggs on top.

4. Cook 10 more minutes until eggs are over medium.

5. Serve each with potatoes and egg. Toast on the side makes a hearty breakfast.

Sausage Egg Roll Ups

Serves: 8

Cooking Time: 20 minutes

Ingredients:

Eggs, 5

Crescent Rolls, 1 can

Sausage Links, 8 precooked

Cheddar Cheese, 4 slices

Salt, ¼ tsp

Pepper, ¼ tsp

Directions:

1. Whisk eggs. Remove small amount to brush tops of rolls. Scramble rest of eggs.

2. Remove crescent rolls and break apart.

3. Add ½ slice of cheese, egg and sausage link to each roll.

4. Begin at large end and roll into shape.

5. Brush with egg mix. Salt and pepper each to taste.

6. Place in cast iron skillet.

7. Bake in 350F preheated oven for 20 minutes.

8. Remove from oven and serve.

Breakfast Mac & Cheese

Serves: 6

Cooking Time: 30 minutes

Ingredients:

Elbow Macaroni, 1 lb., cooked and drained

Sausage, 1 lb., cooked and crumbled

Onion, 1 large, diced

Green Pepper, 1, diced

Garlic Powder, ½ tsp

Butter, 4 Tbsp

Flour, 6 Tbsp

Milk, 4 cups

Colby Jack Cheese, 5 cups

Pepper Jack Cheese, 1 cup

Salt, ¼ tsp

Pepper, ¼ tsp

Eggs, 4

Breakfast Biscuits, cooked and crumbled

Directions:

1. Prepare pasta and drain.

2. Cook sausage in cast iron skillet, remove and drain.

3. Sauté onion, pepper and garlic powder.

4. Add butter to same skillet with flour. Stir constantly.

5. Pour in milk and stir until smooth. Remove from heat and add cheeses, salt and pepper.

6. Add macaroni, sausage and onion pepper mix.

7. Mix eggs, cheese and biscuits. Pour over macaroni mixture.

8. Bake in 375F preheated oven for 30 minutes.

9. Let stand for a few minutes, then serve warm.

Breakfast Enchiladas

Serves: 6

Cooking Time: 10 minutes

Ingredients:

Pork Sausage, 1 lb

Butter, 2 Tbsp

Green Onions, 4 sliced

Cilantro, 2 Tbsp, chopped

Eggs, 14 beaten

Salt, ¾ tsp

Pepper, ½ tsp

Cheese Sauce, 1 jar

Flour Tortillas, 8

Monterey Jack Cheese, 1 cup

Toppings:

Sliced cherry tomatoes, 1 cup

Green Onions, ½ cup sliced

Directions:

1. Prepare sausage, cook and drain.

2. Melt butter in cast iron skillet. Sauté green onions and cilantro. Pour in eggs, salt and pepper.

3. Mix in 1 ½ cups of cheese sauce.

4. Put a small amount of cheese mixture on each tortilla.

5. Roll up and place in cast iron skillet.

6. Pour remaining cheese sauce over filled tortillas.

7. Sprinkle with cheese.

8. Bake in 350F preheated oven for 10 minutes until cheese is melted.

Skillet Breakfast Relish

Serves: 4

Cooking Time: approximately 40 minutes

Ingredients:

Oil, 1 Tbsp

Onions, 1 small, chopped

Garlic, 2 cloves, chopped

Cumin, 1 tsp

Chili powder, 1 tsp

Jalapeno peppers, 2 diced

Diced Tomatoes, 4 cups

Black Beans, 1 can, rinsed and drained

Oregano, 1 tsp

Salt, ¼ tsp

Pepper, ¼ tsp

Cilantro, 1 bunch, chopped

Eggs, 4

Cheese, ½ cup shredded

Directions:

1. Place cast iron skillet on stove, add oil and heat.

2. Sauté onions about 5 minutes.

3. Combine onions with garlic, cumin, chili powder and jalapeno for 1 minute.

4. Put tomatoes, beans, oregano, salt and pepper in skillet and bring to boil.

5. Turn heat down and simmer for 20 minutes.

6. Set aside and stir in cilantro.

7. Make a well in the mixture, add eggs and spoon mixture around eggs.

8. Transfer cast iron skillet to oven and bake at 350F for 8 to 10 minutes.

9. Top with cheese and bake for a few minutes more until cheese is melted.

10. Serve with toast.

Tasty Potato, Pepper & Egg Breakfast

Serves: 6

Cooking Time: 30 minutes

Ingredients:

Potatoes, 3, peeled and shredded

Butter, 1 Tbsp

Vegetable Oil, 2 Tbsp

Bell Pepper, 1, diced

Onion, 1 medium, diced

Garlic, 1 clove, pressed

Salt, ¾ tsp

Eggs, 6 large

Pepper, ¼ tsp

Directions:

1. Cover shredded potatoes with cold water. Let stand 5 minutes, then drain and dry.

2. Add butter to your cast iron skillet and melt. Sauté peppers and onions about 5 minutes. Add garlic, potatoes and ½ tsp. salt. Cook for 10 minutes, stirring often.

3. Make indentations in potato mixture, add an egg to each.

4. Sprinkle with salt and pepper and bake for 14 minutes in 350F preheated oven.

5. Serve warm with biscuits or toast.

Cast Iron Skillet Strata

Serves: 4

Cooking Time: 20 minutes

Ingredients:

Eggs, 6 large

Milk, 1 ½ cups

Cheddar Cheese, 1 cup, shredded

Butter, 4 Tbsp

Onion, 1 diced

Thyme, 1 tsp

Cayenne, ¼ tsp

Garlic Powder, ¼ tsp

Mustard, ¼ tsp

Salt, ¼ tsp

Pepper, ¼ tsp

Bread cubes, 5 cups

Directions:

1. Melt butter in cast iron skillet. Add onions, salt and pepper. Cook about 6 minutes.

2. Add bread cubes, thyme, cayenne, mustard and garlic. Mix to coat.

3. Mix eggs, milk and cheese together.

4. Take pan off heat and fold eggs in with bread mixture.

5. Bake in 425F preheated oven for 14 minutes. Edges will be brown and center puffy.

6. Slice and serve warm.

Yummy Egg, Potato & Sausage

Serves: 8

Cooking Time: 20 minutes

Ingredients:

Sausage, 16 oz. pkg

Frozen Potatoes, 1 bag with peppers and onions

Broccoli, ½ cup, chopped

Eggs, 8, beaten

Milk, ½ cup

Garlic Powder, ¼ tsp

Salt, ¼ tsp

Pepper, ¼ tsp

Cheddar Cheese, 1 cup grated

Directions:

1. Cook sausage in cast iron skillet. Drain and add potatoes with peppers and onions, and broccoli.

2. Mix eggs, milk, garlic powder, salt and pepper. Pour over sausage and potato mixture.

3. Place lid on skillet and reduce heat. Cook for 10 minutes.

4. Uncover and cook for 6 more minutes. Make sure egg mixture is set.

5. Remove from heat and sprinkle with cheese.

6. Serve after cheese has melted.

Cast Iron Skillet Hash

Serves: 4

Cooking Time: 40 minutes

Ingredients:

Olive Oil, 2 Tbsp

Sausage, 1 lb., cooked

Green Pepper, 1 med. chopped

Red Pepper, 1 med. chopped

Onion, 1 small, chopped

Potatoes, 3 large, chopped

Eggs, 4

Salt, 1 tsp

Pepper, 1 tsp

Directions:

1. Cook potatoes in olive oil for 7 minutes. Add green pepper, red pepper, and onion. Continue to cook until tender.

2. Add in sausage. Mix sausage, potatoes, peppers and onions, salt and pepper.

3. Top hash mix with sausage. Cook until eggs are the consistency you would like.

4. Serve with egg on each serving.

Cast Iron Skillet Shepherd's Breakfast

Serves: 8

Cooking Time: 30 minutes

Ingredients:

Bacon, ¾ lb., chopped

Onion, 1 med. chopped

Frozen Shredded Hash Brown potatoes, 1 pkg. thawed

Eggs, 8

Salt, ½ tsp

Pepper, ¼ tsp

Cheddar Cheese, 1 cup, shredded

Directions:

1. Cook bacon and onion over medium heat. Drain and save ½ of bacon grease.

2. Add hash browns and cook, uncovered for 10 minutes.

3. Make dips in the cooked hash browns, add 1 egg per dip.

4. Add salt and pepper to taste.

5. Place lid on skillet and cook for 10 minutes or until eggs are the right consistency.

6. Remove lid and sprinkle with cheddar cheese. Let stand until melted.

7. Serve warm.

Skillet Ham And Cheese Quiche

Serves: 6

Cooking Time: 40 minutes

Ingredients:

Prepared crust, 1, thawed

Butter, 2 Tbsp

Onion, ½, diced

Garlic, 2 cloves, minced

Ham, 2 cups, chopped

Cheddar Cheese, 1 cup, chopped

Dijon Mustard, 1 Tbsp

Eggs, 6

Heavy Cream, ½ to 1 cup

Pepper, 1 tsp

Parsley, 3 Tbsp

Directions:

1. Heat butter and onions until onions are soft.

2. Add ham and garlic and cook for a few minutes.

3. Mix eggs, mustard, cream, cheese and parsley. Add ham mixture to egg mixture.

4. Roll dough into cast iron skillet, add filling and bake in preheated oven of 400F for 40 minutes until set. Allow to cool, then slice and serve.

Cast Iron Skillet Hash Brown Quiche

Serves: 6

Cooking Time: 1 hour

Ingredients:

Potatoes, 5

Salt, ¼ tsp

Pepper, ¼ tsp

Olive Oil, ¼ tsp

Butter, 1 Tbsp., melted.

Bacon, ½ lb. cooked and chopped

Zucchinis, 1 chopped

Onion, 1 chopped

Cheese, 1 cup of your choice

Eggs, 7

Milk, 2 cups

Rosemary, ¼ tsp

Tarragon, ¼ tsp

Directions:

1. Shred potatoes and rinse. Pat dry with towel.

2. Mix potatoes with butter, olive oil, salt and pepper.

3. Place in cast iron skillet and cook in preheated oven of 425F for 30 minutes.

4. Mix eggs, milk, bacon, onion, zucchini, spices and cheese.

5. Pour mixture into prepared hash brown crust.

6. Bake in 375F oven for 30 minutes until set.

7. Slice and serve.

Spicy Breakfast Eggs

Serves: 4

Cooking Time: 15 minutes

Ingredients:

Olive Oil, 4 Tbsp

Onion, 1 medium, chopped

Garlic, 6 cloves, sliced

Jalapeno peppers, 4, seeded and diced

Hot Chili Flakes, 1 tsp

Tomato sauce, 3 cups

Eggs, 8

Pecorino Romano Cheese, ¼ cup, grated

Directions:

1. Heat cast iron skillet over medium heat.

2. Add olive oil, chopped onion, garlic, jalapenos, cheese and chili flakes. Cook about 8 minutes.

3. Mix in tomato sauce and heat until boiling.

4. Crack eggs into tomato sauce.

5. Cook about 7 minutes or until eggs' consistency is to your desire.

6. Remove and serve warm.

Breakfast Sweet Potato, Bacon & Egg

Serves: 4

Cooking Time: 25 minutes

Ingredients:

Sweet Potatoes, 1 ½ lbs., diced

Bacon, 1 lb

Oil, 2 Tbsp

Chipotle Seasoning, 2 Tbsp

Eggs, 4

Directions:

1. Cook bacon in iron skillet for 10 minutes, chop and set aside.

2. Heat oil in cast iron skillet and add sweet potatoes.

3. When sweet potatoes are soft, about 10 minutes, add the bacon in.

4. Add eggs one at a time.

5. Cook for 5 more minutes or until egg whites are set.

6. Remove from heat and season with chipotle seasoning.

7. Serve warm.

Woven Bacon Skillet

Serves: 2

Cooking Time: 35 minutes

Ingredients:

Bacon, 6 slices

Eggs, 2

Cherry Tomatoes, 8

Parsley, 1 tsp

Directions:

1. Place bacon in cast iron skillet as a woven pattern.

2. Bake in preheated 400F oven for 10 minutes and flip over then bake other side 10 more minutes.

3. Pat dry and place in cast iron skillet.

4. Place eggs in the center of the bacon, spread tomatoes and sprinkle on parsley.

5. Bake 10 to 15 more minutes.

6. Remove and enjoy!

Baked Ham & Cheese Omelet

Serves: 4

Cooking Time: 35 minutes

Ingredients:

Butter, 2 Tbsp

Onion, ½, chopped

Green Bell Pepper, ½, chopped

Ham, 1 cup, chopped

Eggs, 8

Milk, ¼ cup

Cheddar Cheese, ½ cup

Pepper, ¼ tsp

Salt, ¼ tsp

Directions:

1. Grease cast iron skillet and set aside.

2. In another skillet, melt butter, add onions and bell pepper. Cook for 5 minutes until soft.

3. Add ham and cook for 5 more minutes.

4. Blend eggs and milk. Add cheese, ham mix, salt and pepper.

5. Pour into greased cast iron skillet.

6. Bake in oven preheated 400F for 20 minutes. Serve warm.

Cast Iron Skillet Bacon Cheese Biscuits

Serves: 4

Cooking Time: 20 minutes

Ingredients:

Biscuits, 1 can of 8

Bacon, 1 lb., cooked and chopped

Cheese, 1 cup, shredded

Directions:

1. Preheat oven to 400F.

2. Grease cast iron skillet well.

3. Place biscuits in skillet, add cooked bacon on top.

4. Top with cheddar cheese.

5. Cook for 20 minutes until cheese has browned some.

6. Remove and enjoy.

Bacon Spinach Breakfast Casserole

Serves: 8

Cooking Time: 45 minutes

Ingredients:

Oil, 1 Tbsp

French bread, 8 to 10 slices

Butter, 1 Tbsp

Bacon, 6 slices

Spinach, 5 oz

Onion, 1 medium, diced

Eggs, 6

Milk, 1 ½ cup

Cheddar Cheese, 1 ½ cup

Salt, ¼ tsp

Pepper, ¼ tsp

Directions:

1. Toast bread and spread with butter. Cube the bread.

2. Cook the bacon, drain and chop. Leave the drippings in skillet.

3. Add onions, cook for 5 minutes, then add spinach.

4. Remove from heat.

5. Beat eggs, milk, cheese, salt and pepper.

6. Add bacon, bread, spinach and onions. Coat well.

7. Oil cast iron skillet. Pour bread mix into skillet.

8. Pour egg mixture over bread and bacon mix.

9. Bake in 350F preheated oven for 45 minutes.

10. Slice and serve warm.

Loaded Baked Potato Breakfast Skillet

Serves: 4

Cooking Time: 20 minutes

Ingredients:

Potato, 1 large, cubed

Salt, ½ tsp

Vegetable Oil, 1 Tbsp

Bacon, 5 slices, cooked

Green Onion, 2 Tbs., chopped

Cheddar Cheese, ½ cup

Eggs, 4

Milk, ½ cup

Sour Cream, 1 Tbsp

Pepper, ½ tsp

Directions:

1. Beat eggs, milk, sour cream, salt and pepper together.

2. Cook potatoes in oil in heated cast iron skillet.

3. Remove and add bacon and green onions.

4. Pour egg mix over skillet mix.

5. Bake in 350F preheated oven for 20 minutes.

6. Remove and serve warm.

Seasoned Sausage, Egg & Cheese Breakfast Bread

Serves: 12

Cooking Time: 40 minutes

Ingredients:

Cooking Spray

Canned Biscuits, 3 cans

Eggs, 8

Milk 1 Tbsp.

Mustard, 1 tsp

Salt, ¼ tsp

Pepper, ¼ tsp

Sausage, 1 lb

Cheese, 1 pkg., shredded

Directions:

1. Cook sausage and drain. Combine eggs, milk, mustard, salt and pepper.

2. Break biscuits into bite-size pieces. Coat biscuit pieces in egg mixture.

3. Spray cast iron skillet with cooking spray and place biscuit pieces in even layers.

4. Pour rest of egg mixture over the biscuits. Spread sausage over biscuits and sprinkle with cheese.

5. Bake in 350F preheated oven for 40 minutes. Remove, let cool a little, then pull apart and enjoy.

Cast Iron Skillet Biscuits &Sausage Gravy

Serves: 6

Cooking Time: 1 hour

Ingredients:

Sausage, 1 lb. any brand

Country Gravy Mix, 1 pkg

Cheddar Cheese, 1 cup

Eggs, 3

Milk, ½ cup

Cream, 1 pint

Pepper, ¼ tsp

Salt, ¼ tsp

Onion, 1 tsp., minced

Biscuits, 1 can

Bacon, 8 slices

Directions:

1. Cook sausage and bacon. Set aside.

2. Spray cast iron skillet.

3. Cut biscuits into bite-size pieces and layer in skillet.

4. Spread sausage and crumble bacon over biscuits.

5. Sprinkle with cheese.

6. Mix eggs, milk, cream, pepper, salt, and onions.

7. Pour over biscuits, sausage and bacon.

8. Mix gravy mix and pour over all.

9. It can be refrigerated overnight or cooked the same day.

10. Cook in 350F preheated oven for 1 hour.

11. Remove after top is browned lightly.

Sausage And Crescent Roll Bake

Serves: 6

Cooking Time: 20 minutes

Ingredients:

Sausage, 1 lb

Crescent Rolls, 1 can

Cheese, 1 cup

Eggs, 5

Milk, ¼ cup

Oregano, 1 tsp

Salt, ½ tsp

Pepper, ¼ tsp

Directions:

1. Cook sausage and drain.

2. Spread crescent rolls on bottom of cast iron skillet.

3. Spread sausage over crescent rolls. Sprinkle with cheese.

4. Mix eggs, milk, oregano, salt and pepper.

5. Pour mixture over crescent roll, sausage and cheese.

6. Bake at 400F preheated oven for 20 minutes until crust is browned.

7. Remove and serve.

Ham And Sausage Hash Brown Egg Bake

Serves: 4

Cooking Time: 30 minutes

Ingredients:

Italian Sausage, 4 oz., cooked

Ham, 2 cups, chopped

Eggs, 4

Milk, ½ cup

Garlic Powder, ¼ tsp

Refrigerated Hash Browns, 1 bag

Cheese, ½ cup shredded

Green Onions, 2 Tbsp., chopped

Directions:

1. Sauté ham and sausage together.

2. Mix eggs, milk and garlic powder together.

3. Oil cast iron skillet and add hash browns, spread evenly.

4. Pour ½ of egg mixture over hash browns. Sprinkle with some of the cheese.

5. Spread ham and sausage over egg mixture. Add other half of egg mixture and cheese.

6. Bake in 350F preheated oven for 30 minutes.

7. Remove and sprinkle green onions over dish and serve.

Gingerbread French Toast Breakfast Bake
Serves: 6

Cooking Time: 30 minutes

Ingredients:

Cooking Spray

Texas Toast, 12 slices

Butter, ½ stick

Eggs, 3

Milk, ½ cup

Maple Syrup, ¼ cup

Molasses, ¼ cup

Cinnamon, 1 tsp

Ginger, 1 tsp

Allspice, 1 tsp

Nutmeg, 1 tsp

Cloves, ½ tsp. ground

Confectioners' sugar to dust

Directions:

1. Spray 2 cast iron skillets with cooking spray.

2. Place bread slices in pan.

3. Melt butter and add eggs, milk, syrup, molasses, cinnamon, ginger, allspice, nutmeg and cloves. Mix well.

4. Pour mixture over bread in both skillets.

5. Cover with foil and refrigerate 4 hours.

6. Remove foil and bake in 350F preheated oven for 30 minutes.

7. Remove and sprinkle with powdered sugar.

8. Serve with syrup on the side.

Cast Iron Skillet Apple Pancakes

Serves: 4

Cooking Time: 5 to 10 minutes per pancake

Ingredients:

Eggs, 2

Milk, 1 ½ cups

All-Purpose Flour, 2 cups

Baking Powder, 1 tsp

Salt, ½ tsp

Sugar, ¼ cup

Apples, 3 medium, peeled and chopped

Vegetable Oil, 1 Tbsp

Directions:

1. Mix eggs, milk, flour, baking powder, salt and sugar. Blend well.

2. Add apples and combine.

3. Heat oil in cast iron skillet.

4. Pour mix in for pancake. Let brown and flip.

5. Continue to do this for each pancake.

6. Serve with butter and syrup.

Cast Iron Skillet French Toast

Serves: 4

Cooking Time: 10 to 15 minutes per Toast

Ingredients:

French bread, 8 slices, 1 inch thick

Eggs, 3

Milk, 1 cup

Oil, 1 Tbsp

Powdered Sugar for sprinkling

Syrup, 1 cup

Directions:

1. Heat oil in cast iron skillet.

2. Mix eggs and milk well.

3. Dip each slice of bread in egg mixture and coat well.

4. Cook in heated skillet until eggs have set up and browned well.

5. Remove and sprinkle powdered sugar on top.

6. Serve alone or with syrup on the side.

Butter Buttermilk Biscuits

Serves: 4 to 6

Cooking Time: 20 minutes

Ingredients:

Oil, for greasing pan

Self-Rising Flour, 2 cups

Salt, ½ tsp

Sugar, 1 tsp

Shortening, 3 Tbsp

Butter, ½ stick, cold

Buttermilk, ¾ cup

Directions:

1. Cut butter and shortening into flour. Add milk, salt and sugar. Combine until able to make a ball.

2. Place on floured board and knead a little.

3. Roll out with floured rolling pin.

4. Cut and place in oiled cast iron skillet.

5. Bake at 400F for 20 minutes until lightly browned.

6. Serve warm with butter and preserves.

Lemon Blueberry Scones

Serves: 6

Cooking Time: 30 minutes

Ingredients:

All-purpose flour, 2 cups

Baking Powder, 2 tsp

Sugar, 4 Tbsp

Salt, ¼ tsp

Butter, ½ stick, cold

Blueberries, 1 cup

Lemon Zest of 1 lemon

Milk, 1 cup

Vanilla Extract, 1 tsp

Glaze:

Powdered Sugar, ½ cup

Lemon Juice, 5 Tbsp

Directions:

1. Mix sifted flour, baking powder, sugar and salt.

2. Cut butter into flour mixture.

3. Add ½ cup of blueberries and lemon zest. Pour in milk and vanilla and combine.

4. Place dough on floured board.

5. Knead and press into sprayed cast iron skillet. Sprinkle sugar on top.

6. Bake in 375F preheated oven for 30 minutes.

7. Prepare glaze and set aside.

8. Remove and spread glaze on scones while warm.

9. Slice as you would pie and serve.

Cinnamon Rolls Skillet
Serves: 6 to 8

Cooking Time: 35 minutes

Ingredients:

Prepared dough, 2 pkgs.

Butter, 1 stick, melted

Sugar, 1 cup

Cinnamon, 3 tsp

Glaze:

Cream Cheese, 4 oz., room temp

Butter, 4 Tbsp. melted

Confectioners' Sugar, 2 cups

Hot milk, 4 Tbsp

Orange Extract, 2 tsp

Orange Zest, 1 tsp

Directions:

1. Let dough rise in warm area for 1 hour.

2. Roll dough out to rectangles.

3. Spread melted butter over the rectangles.

4. Mix sugar and cinnamon. Sprinkle over buttered dough.

5. Roll each rectangle tightly. Cut into even rolls.

6. Place in sprayed cast iron skillet and cook in 400F preheated oven for 35 minutes.

7. While rolls are cooking, mix cream cheese, butter, confectioners' sugar, milk, orange extract and zest.

8. Remove and spread glaze over cinnamon rolls while hot.

9. Serve warm.

Sugared Cinnamon Pecan Rolls

Serves: 12

Cooking Time: 25 minutes

Ingredients:

Cooking Spray

Pecans, 1 cup chopped

Hot Roll Mix, 1 pkg

Butter, 1 stick softened

Brown Sugar, 1 cup

Powdered Sugar, 1 cup

Cinnamon, 2 tsp

Milk, 2 Tbsp

Vanilla Extract, 1 tsp

Directions:

1. Toast pecans in pan for 5 minutes, stirring while toasting.

2. Prepare roll mix. Roll into rectangle.

3. Spread rolls with butter.

4. Mix brown sugar and cinnamon. Spread over butter.

5. Spread pecans over brown sugar and cinnamon.

6. Beginning at end, roll up tightly.

7. Cut into 12 rolls and place in sprayed cast iron skillet. Let rise.

8. Bake in preheated oven of 375F for 30 minutes.

9. Mix powdered sugar, milk and vanilla while rolls are cooking.

10. Spread mixture over hot rolls and serve.

Light Blueberry Biscuits

Serves: 6

Cooking Time: 20 minutes

Ingredients:

Oil, for greasing cast iron skillet

Self-rising flour, 2 cups

Butter, 1 stick

Shortening, 3 Tbsp

Buttermilk, ¾ cup

Frozen Blueberries, 1 cup

Butter, ½ stick, melted

Sauce:

Powdered Sugar, 1 cup

Milk, 3 Tbsp

Vanilla, ½ tsp

Directions:

1. Mix flour, butter, shortening and buttermilk. Mix well and turn out on floured board.

2. Knead slightly. Add blueberries on top and knead into dough.

3. Roll out and cut with biscuit cutter.

4. Oil cast iron skillet. Place biscuits touching each other in skillet.

5. Bake at 400F preheated oven for 20 minutes.

6. Prepare sauce of powdered sugar, milk and vanilla while biscuits are cooking.

7. A few minutes before biscuits are done, remove and pour sauce over them.

8. Put back in oven and cook for remaining time.

9. Serve warm.

Twin Berry Puff Pancakes
Serves: 4

Cooking Time: 20 minutes

Ingredients:

Eggs, 4 large

Milk, 1 cup

Self-rising flour, 1 cup

Sugar, ¼ cup

Lemon zest, ½ tsp

Salt, ¼ tsp

Butter, 2 Tbsp

Blueberries, ½ cup

Raspberries, ½ cup

Directions:

1. Mix eggs, milk, flour, sugar, lemon zest and salt. Combine well.

2. Melt butter in cast iron skillet.

3. Pour batter into skillet, sprinkle berries on top.

4. Bake in 400F preheated oven for 20 minutes or until light brown.

5. Slice and serve with topping of choice.

Cast Iron Maple Bacon French Toast
Serves: 10

Cooking Time: 40 minutes

Ingredients:

Cooking Oil, 2 Tbsp

Eggs, 8

Half and half cream, 2 cups

Milk, 1 cup

Sugar, 1 Tbsp

Brown Sugar, 1 Tbsp

Vanilla Extract, 1 tsp.3

Cinnamon, ½ tsp

Nutmeg, ¼ tsp

Salt, ¼ tsp

French Bread, 1 loaf cut into slices

Topping:

Bacon, 6 slices, cooked and crumbled

Butter, 1 cup

Brown Sugar, 1 cup

Pecans, ½ cup, toasted and chopped

Corn Syrup, 2 Tbsp

Cinnamon, 1 tsp

Nutmeg, ½ tsp

Cloves, ¼ tsp

Maple Syrup, 1 cup

Directions:

1. Combine eggs, cream, milk, sugar, brown sugar, vanilla, cinnamon, nutmeg and salt. Mix well.

2. Grease 2 to 3 cast iron skillets. Dip bread in egg mixture and arrange in skillets. Refrigerate for 1 hour.

3. Mix bacon, butter, brown sugar, pecans, corn syrup, cinnamon, nutmeg, cloves and maple syrup.

4. Crumble topping mix over bread.

5. Bake, uncovered, in a 350F preheated oven for 40 minutes until middle is done.

6. Let stand, then drizzle with syrup.

Cast Iron Skillet Coffee Cake

Serves: 10

Cooking Time: 30 minutes

Ingredients:

Topping:

Walnuts, 1 cup, chopped

All-purpose flour, ⅔ cup

Sugar, ⅓ cup

Brown Sugar, ⅓ cup

Cinnamon, 2 tsp

Salt, 1 tsp

Butter, 5 Tbsp., melted

Coffee Cake:

Butter, 5 Tbsp

Eggs, 2 at room temp.

All-purpose flour, 2 cups

Baking Powder, 1 tsp

Soda, 1 tsp

Salt, 1 tsp

Sour Cream, 1 ½ cup

Lemon Zest, 1 Tbsp

Directions:

1. Combine nuts, flour, sugars, cinnamon and salt. Stir in butter. Break up in pan and set aside.

2. Mix butter and sugar, add eggs, one at a time, and mix.

3. Combine flour, baking powder, soda, salt. Mix and add to sour cream and lemon zest.

4. Grease cast iron skillet and pour flour mixture in.

5. Crumble topping evenly on cake.

6. Bake in 350F preheated oven and cook for 30 minutes.

7. Remove and cool, slice and serve.

Apple Pie Breakfast Bake
Serves: 8

Cooking Time: 35 minutes

Ingredients:

French Loaf dough, 1 refrigerated

Butter, 1 cup

Apple Pie Filling, 1 can

Sweetened Condensed Milk, 1 can

Apple Pie Spice, 1 tsp

Vanilla, 1 tsp

Maple Syrup, 1 cup, warmed

Directions:

1. Cube one of the French loaf dough.

2. In buttered cast iron skillet, layer bread cubes and apple pie filling.

3. Combine sweetened condensed milk, apple pie spice and vanilla.

4. Pour over bread cubes and apple pie filling.

5. Bake in 325F preheated oven for 35 minutes.

6. Cool and serve with warm maple syrup.

Turtle Cinnamon Rolls
Serves: 8

Cooking Time: 25 minutes

Ingredients:

Cinnamon Roll Dough, 1 can, with icing

Chocolate Sauce, 1 jar

Caramel Sauce, 1 jar

Pecan Halves, 24

Directions:

1. Arrange rolls in cast iron skillet.

2. Bake in 375F preheated oven for 15 minutes until brown.

3. Sprinkle chocolate sauce on in zigzags. Do the same with the caramel sauce.

4. Place two pecan halves on each cinnamon roll.

5. Cool before serving.

Cast Iron Skillet Cheese Danish
Serves: 8

Cooking Time: 20 minutes

Ingredients:

Cream Cheese, 8 oz.

Sugar, 1/3 cup

Egg Yolks, 2 large at room temp.

Ricotta Cheese, 2 Tbsp

Vanilla Extract, 1 tsp

Salt, ¼ tsp

Lemon zest of 2 lemons

Frozen Puff Pastry, 2 sheets, thawed

Egg, 1 with a Tbsp. of water, beaten for egg wash

Directions:

1. Spray cast iron skillet and set aside.

2. Mix cream cheese and sugar together.

3. Add egg yolks, ricotta cheese, vanilla, salt and lemon zest and mix well.

4. Place 1 sheet of puff pastry on floured board and roll gently into a rectangle. Cut into squares.

5. Place 1 spoonful of mixture on the pastry. Roll out another puff pastry and cut into squares.

6. Place 1 square on top of each pastry with mixture. Pinch edges to seal.

7. Brush with egg wash.

8. Bake in 400F preheated oven for 20 minutes.

9. Remove and serve warm or cold.

Fruit And Oatmeal Bake

Serves: 6

Cooking Time: 40 minutes

Ingredients:

Oats, 2 cups

Brown Sugar, ⅓ cup

Baking Powder, 1 tsp

Cinnamon, 1 tsp

Salt, ½ tsp

Walnuts, 1 cup

Blueberries, 1 cup

Chocolate Chips, ½ cup

Milk, 2 cups

Egg, 1 large

Butter, 3 Tbsp., melted

Vanilla, 1 Tbsp

Banana, 1 sliced

Directions:

1. Preheat oven to 350F.

2. Combine all ingredients and pour into greased cast iron skillet.

3. Bake for 40 minutes. Serve while warm.

Pancake And Sausage Casserole
Serves: 6

Cooking Time: 45 minutes

Ingredients:

Cooking Spray

Sausage, 1 lb

Self-rising flour, 4 cups

Sugar, ¼ cup

Brown Sugar, ¼ cup

Eggs, 4

Milk, 2 ½ cups

Oil, ¼ cup

Vanilla Extract, 1 tsp

Directions:

1. Spray cast iron skillet with cooking spray.

2. Prepare sausage, crumble and drain.

3. Mix flour, sugar, brown sugar, eggs, milk, oil and vanilla extract together. Combine until smooth. Add sausage and mix well.

4. Bake in 375F preheated oven for 45 minutes or until toothpick comes out clean.

5. Remove and serve with syrup.

Easy Cast Iron Doughnuts

Serves: 8

Cooking Time: 15 minutes

Ingredients:

Biscuits, 1 can

Oil, 1 ½ cup

Sugar, 1 cup

Cinnamon, 1 cup

Directions:

1. Heat oil in skillet over medium heat.

2. Shape a hole in the middle of each biscuit.

3. Drop in hot skillet and cook on each side.

4. Remove and dip in sugar and cinnamon mixture.

5. Lay on paper towel to cool.

6. Serve warm or cool.

Easy Glazed Doughnut Holes

Serves: 6

Cooking Time: 5 minutes

Ingredients:

Glaze:

Powdered sugar, 1 ½ cups

Milk, 4 Tbsp

Vanilla Extract, 2 tsp

Doughnut Holes:

Oil, 5 cups

Milk, 1 cup

Egg, 1 large

Flour, 2 cups self-rising

Sugar, 2 Tbsp

Butter, ½ stick, melted

Directions:

1. Heat oil in large cast iron skillet.

2. Combine flour, egg, milk, sugar and butter until blended.

3. Place on floured board and roll into 24 round balls.

4. Drop each into hot oil, turning to brown evenly.

5. Remove and let drain.

6. Prepare glaze by mixing all the ingredients.

7. Pour glaze over doughnut holes.

8. Set aside and let cool until glaze has set.

9. Enjoy!

Cast Iron Apple Fritters

Serves: 4 to 6

Cooking Time: 15 minutes

Ingredients:

Vegetable Oil, 3 cups for cooking

Self-rising flour, 1 ½ cups

Sugar, 1 Tbsp

Milk, ⅔ cup

Eggs, 2, beaten

Oil, 1 Tbsp

Apples, 3 cups, peeled, cored and chopped

Cinnamon, 1 cup

Directions:

1. Heat oil in cast iron skillet.

2. Combine flour and sugar. Add the milk, eggs and oil. Combine well.

3. Mix apples in flour mixture.

4. Drop by spoonfuls into hot oil.

5. Cook about 5 minutes on each side until lightly browned.

6. Remove and drain.

7. Coat with cinnamon and sugar.

Cast Iron Jelly Doughnuts

Serves: 8

Cooking Time: 10 minutes

Ingredients:

Yeast, 2 pkgs. active

Warm Water, ½ cup

Milk, ½ cup warm

Butter, ⅓ cup, softened

Sugar, 1 ⅓ cups

Egg Yolks, 3

Salt, 1 tsp

All-purpose flour, 3 ¾ cups

Jelly, 3 Tbsp

Egg White, 1 lightly beaten

Oil, 3 cups

Directions:

1. Dissolve yeast in warm water; add milk, butter, ⅓ cup of sugar, egg yolks, salt and flour. Mix until smooth and then fold in the egg whites gently.

2. Cover and let rise.

3. Punch down dough, place on floured board. Divide into 2 halves.

4. Roll each half about ¼ inch in thickness.

5. Cut with biscuit cutter. Place 1 spoonful of jelly on round. Top with remaining rounds. Pinch edges to seal.

6. Cover and let rise about 45 minutes.

7. Heat oil in cast iron skillet.

8. Drop each into hot oil. Let brown on each side about 5 minutes.

9. Remove and drain.

10. Roll in sugar and set on plate.

Popover Pancake
Serves: 4

Cooking Time: 25 minutes

Ingredients:

Eggs, 4 large, beaten

Milk, 1 cup

All-purpose flour, 1 cup

Butter, 1 ½ sticks, melted

Salt, ¼ tsp

Orange Marmalade, 3 Tbsp

Butter, 3 Tbsp

Lemon juice, 1 Tbsp

Frozen sliced peaches, 1 pkg.

Blueberries, 1 cup frozen

Directions:

1. Mix eggs, milk, flour, butter and salt. Blend well.

2. Preheat greased skillet in 425F oven.

3. Pour mixture into skillet. Bake for 25 minutes.

4. Mix marmalade, butter and lemon juice in pan. Boil.

6. Mix in peaches and cook for 3 minutes.

7. Pour on pancake and spread with blueberries. Serve immediately.

Cornmeal Pancake With Sausage & Maple Syrup
Serves: 4

Cooking Time: 40 minutes

Ingredients:

Yellow cornmeal, ½ cup

All-purpose flour, ½ cup

Sugar, 1 Tbsp

Salt, ¾ tsp

Baking Powder, ½ tsp

Milk, 1 cup

Eggs, 2 large

Butter, ¼ stick

Sausage Links, 14

Maple Syrup, 3 Tbsp., plus more

Directions:

1. Mix cornmeal, flour, sugar, salt and baking powder.

2. Blend in milk and eggs. Mix well.

3. Cook sausage in butter and set to side. Remix batter and pour into cast iron skillet.

4. Place sausage on top of pancake and drizzle with maple syrup.

5. Bake in 375F preheated oven for 15 minutes. Cut and pour maple syrup over each slice.

Potatoes, Bacon And Cheese

Serves: 4

Cooking Time: 20 minutes

Ingredients:

Baked Potatoes, 4

Onion, ½ sliced

Salt, ¼ tsp

Pepper, ¼ tsp

Garlic Powder, ½ tsp

Bacon, 1 lb. cooked and chopped

Cheddar cheese, 2 cups

Eggs, 6

Milk, ½ cup

Directions:

1. Preheat oven to 400F and place skillet in oven.

2. Melt butter in skillet and sauté onion, bell pepper and garlic. Add salt and pepper.

3. Mix eggs and milk well.

4. Remove skillet and make layers of the ingredients: potatoes, bacon, onion, cheese, egg mixture.

5. Cook for 20 minutes until eggs puff up.

6. Serve immediately.

BOOK 2

CAST IRON SKILLET COOKBOOK: VOL.2 LUNCH RECIPES

Introduction

What's for lunch? Anything you want to cook in a cast iron skillet. The choices are endless for great lunch ideas. If you want a light lunch, all you will need is bread, meat, cheese and butter. Pasta is a great lunch idea in your cast iron skillet.

Years ago, farmers ate breakfast, lunch and dinner cooked in a cast iron skillet. It was well used on the farm. Then it seemed the cast iron skillet did not get a great reputation for a while. Stainless steel and non-stick skillets were the way of the future. They are great also. However, the discovery of the cast iron skillet has made a comeback with many cooks. It holds heat great and has easy cleanup potential. The rediscovery of this skillet has put it back on the market and it is now competitive with other cookware.

My grandmother used to keep a well-greased cast iron skillet on the stove at all times. Add a little butter or oil to the skillet and whip up a mean grilled cheese sandwich. Many grilled cheese sandwiches were cooked at Grandma's. She made cornbread, pies, fried chicken and many other favorites in her cast iron skillet. The tasty meals will long be remembered.

Be sure to learn the proper way of caring for your cast iron skillet. Oiling the skillet is the main thing to do to maintain it. If proper care is taken of the skillet, it can last for ages. Skillets are usually handed down through the ages. Auctions are a good place to find them for a reasonable price. Thrift stores and yard sales have many of them also.

If you are a homebody, cooking in your cast iron skillet will be a must. All three meals of the day can be made in this skillet. The lunch will be an easy task. You can create sandwiches, omelets, stir fry and many more tasty treats. If you are on a diet, cooking the meat almost oil free is an advantage in the cast iron skillet. Your skillet should be oiled at all times which makes less sticking with foods.

Your cast iron skillet is the perfect item to have in your kitchen. You are able to fry, bake, sear, sauté and more. The more you fry and bake in it the better you skillet is seasoned. The heat will radiate from your cast iron skillet. They are free of chemical coatings and will last a lifetime, yours or your children's.

Acidic foods are not always great to use in your cast iron skillet. Tomato sauce, wine and citrus can cause the dish to taste metallic. If it is a quick dish, it could be ok. Never store a tomato based dish in cast iron. It will leave your skillet spotty after cleanup.

Whether you are making fried chicken or grilled cheese, your cast iron skillet carries you through. This is the main, if not the only, skillet you should need. It is basically indestructible. It may be a little heavy, but when your recipe calls for a heavy skillet, this is the one.

Think of all the traditional recipes and how they can be incorporated in the cast iron skillet. Lasagna, nachos, potatoes, corn bread and all vegetables and side dishes can be prepared in a cast iron skillet. Cook in your skillet a lot, the more you cook, the better your foods will taste in it. Cooking in cast iron skillets does not limit you to traditional dishes. The dishes and recipes are limitless. Many different cuisines can be cooked in the cast iron skillet.

Home-style cooking is symbolized in the cast iron skillet. Cast iron cooking is slowly growing in popularity. Basic traditions are once again becoming the new traditions. A well seasoned cast iron skillet takes time. It improves each time you use it. Well oiled skillets will become darker in time. Cast iron skillets have much to offer modern-day cooks. Create new recipes your family will love. It's easy to use, versatile, and durable. It looks great with your other cookware.

The cast iron skillet is comfortable in the kitchen or camping. It is a vital tool in camping. Most of the recipes cooked at home can be cooked over a campfire. What better utensil to have over a campfire than a sturdy cast iron skillet. Unlock the secrets of cooking.

Create some adventure in cooking. Most chefs will tell you that cooking in cast iron makes food taste great. Go ahead and try it! Whether you are at home or camping, just make the great dishes that your family loves. Mealtimes are great to catch up with everyone's day and share your love by cooking great dishes.

Go shopping for your skillet; invest in some oil and some great food to prepare in it. You will be an expert in no time!

CAST IRON SKILLET LUNCH RECIPES

Tasty Buffalo Chicken Quesadillas

Serves: 4

Cooking Time: 10 minutes

Ingredients:

Wheat Wraps, 4

Blue Cheese, 4 Tbsp

Cheddar Cheese, ½ cup

Hot Sauce, ¼ cup

Cooked Chicken, 1 ½ cup shredded

Ranch Dressing, 4 Tbsp

Butter Spray

Directions:

1. Spray cast iron skillet with butter spray. Place on skillet on medium heat.

2. Place a tortilla in skillet when hot.

3. Mix shredded chicken with hot sauce.

4. Place cheddar cheese on one half of tortilla, add chicken mix and blue cheese, and top again with cheddar cheese.

5. Fold tortilla in half. Flip and toast other side.

6. Serve with ranch dressing.

7. Do the same to the other 3 tortillas.

Buttermilk Chicken Tender

Serves: 6

Cooking Time: 30 minutes

Ingredients:

Chicken Tenders, 3 lb.

Buttermilk, ¼ cup, plus extra for soaking chicken

All-purpose flour, 3 cups

Seasoning Salt, 3 tsp

Vegetable Oil, 1 to 2 cups

Directions:

1. Heat oil on medium heat in cast iron skillet.

2. Soak chicken tenders in buttermilk.

3. Mix flour, buttermilk and seasoning together.

4. Dip each soaked chicken tender in flour mixture and place in heated oil.

5. Cook for 30 minutes, turning every 10 minutes in order to get evenly brown.

6. Makes a great lunch by itself or chop and add to salad.

Cast Iron Skillet Chicken Ranch Pockets

Serves: 6

Cooking Time: 20 minutes

Ingredients:

Crescent Rolls, 2 cans

Chicken, 2 cups, pre-cooked and diced

Bacon, 1 cup, cooked and chopped

Cheddar Cheese, 2 cups, shredded

Ranch Dressing, ½ cup

Directions:

1. Unroll crescent rolls and seal the perforations.

2. Cut in half and then in quarters.

3. Mix chicken, bacon and cheese

4. Place dressing on each rectangle.

5. Place chicken mixture on each rectangle.

6. Pull dough up over the filling and seal the edges.

7. Bake in cast iron skillet at 375F for 20 minutes or until brown.

8. Serve warm or can be reheated.

Cast Iron Skillet Chicken Avocado Burritos
Serves: 4

Cooking time: 15 minutes

Ingredients:

Chicken, 2 cups, cooked and shredded

Cheese, 1 cup shredded

Avocado, 1, diced

Cilantro, 2 Tbsp., chopped

Tortillas, 4 large

Sour Cream, 4 Tbsp

Oil, 1 Tbsp

Directions:

1. Heat oil in cast iron skillet over medium heat.

2. Combine chicken, cheese, cilantro and avocado.

3. Spread sour cream on each tortilla.

4. Add mixture over the sour cream and roll tortilla.

5. Place in heated oil, cook for 5 minutes on each side until tortillas are browned.

6. Serve warm.

Cheddar Ranch Chicken Burgers

Serves: 4

Cooking Time: 15 to 20 minutes

Ingredients:

Oil, ¼ cup

Chicken, 1 lb. ground

Bread Crumbs, ¼ cup

Panko Bread crumbs, ½ cup

Dried onion flakes, 1 Tbsp.

Seasoned Salt, 1 tsp

Garlic Powder, 1 tsp

Ranch dressing mix, 1 pkg

Cheddar Cheese, 4 slices

Butter, 2 Tbsp

Hamburger Buns, 4

Directions:

1. Heat oil in cast iron skillet over medium heat.

2. Combine chicken, both types of bread crumbs, onion flakes, salt, garlic powder and ranch dressing pack. Combine well and form into patties.

3. Place patties in heated oil and cook for 20 minutes, flipping every 5 minutes until evenly browned.

4. Spread butter on top and bottom of each bun. Broil for 3 minutes.

5. Remove buns, place one patty on each and top with cheese.

6. Serve with tomatoes, lettuce and onions for burgers.

Coconut Chicken Skillet

Serves: 4

Cooking Time: 30 minutes

Ingredients:

Chicken Tenders, 1 ½ lb. cooked

Eggs, 2

Pepper, ½ tsp

Salt, 1 tsp

Flour, ½ cup

Coconut Oil, 4 cups

Shredded Coconut, 1 cup of unsweetened

Panko Crumbs, 4 cup

Directions:

1. Heat coconut oil in cast iron skillet over medium heat.

2. Mix coconut and bread crumbs together. Add flour, salt and pepper, blend well.

3. Whisk egg and blend well.

4. Dip each chicken tender in egg, then in coconut mixture.

5. Place in heated coconut oil. Cook for 30 minutes, turning at intervals.

6. When chicken is browned, drain on paper towel.

7. Serve with sauces of your choice.

Cast Iron Skillet Blackened Chicken Fajitas
Serves: 4

Cooking Time: 20 minutes

Ingredients:

Chicken Breasts, 4 boneless

Fajita Seasoning, ⅓ cup

Salt, 1 tsp

Onions, 1 medium, sliced long ways

Bell Peppers, 3 large, seeds removed and sliced

Canola Oil, 2 Tbsp

Rice, 1 small box, cooked

Lime, 1 wedged, for side

Directions:

1. Cover chicken breast with fajita seasoning and salt.

2. Heat 1 Tbsp. of oil in cast iron skillet over medium heat.

3. Sauté onions and peppers. Remove and set aside, covered.

4. Add 1 Tbsp. of oil and place chicken breasts in heated oil.

5. Cook for 10 minutes until brown. Cover and place in 350F preheated oven for 10 more minutes.

6. Cook rice and place on plate. Slice chicken breasts and lay on rice.

7. Place pepper and onions on top of the chicken breasts.

8. Serve with warm tortillas and limes on the side.

Cast Iron Skillet Baked Chicken Breasts
Serves: 2

Cooking Time: 30 minutes

Ingredients:

Cooking Spray

Chicken Breasts, 2 Boneless, pounded

White Vinegar, 2 Tbsp

Olive Oil, 1 tsp

Onion Powder, ½ tsp

Garlic Powder, ½ tsp

Pepper, ½ tsp

Parsley Flakes, 1 tsp.

Directions:

1. Combine olive oil, vinegar, onion powder, garlic powder, pepper and parsley flakes.

2. Place chicken in mixture and marinate for 1 hour.

3. Spray cast iron skillet with cooking spray and place the chicken breasts in the skillet.

4. Place in 375F preheated oven and bake for 30 minutes until chicken is browned.

5. Remove and serve with nice side salad for a filling lunch.

Gnocchi Chicken Skillet

Serves: 4

Cooking Time: 20 minutes

Ingredients:

Potato Gnocchi, 1 pkg.

Chicken, 1 lb., ground

Onion, ½ cup, chopped

Olive Oil, 2 Tbsp

Spaghetti Sauce, 1 jar

Salt, ¼ tsp

Oregano, ½ tsp

Parmesan Cheese, ½ cup

Directions:

1. Heat cast iron skillet over medium heat.

2. Add chicken and olive oil until chicken is brown. Drain.

3. Prepare gnocchi according to package directions.

4. Stir spaghetti sauce in with chicken, gnocchi, onion, salt and oregano.

5. Spread parmesan cheese over top and serve.

Skillet Chicken & Red Potatoes

Serves: 4

Cooking Time: 30

Ingredients:

Olive Oil, 6 Tbsp., divided

Butter, 2 Tbsp

Carrots, 1 cup, chopped

Potatoes, 2 cups, red

Chicken Breasts, 2 ½ cup boneless

Lemons, 2

Garlic, 1 tsp. minced

Salt, ¼ tsp

Lemon Pepper, ½ tsp

Paprika, ¼ tsp

Parsley, to garnish

Directions:

1. Heat butter and 2 Tbsp. of olive oil in skillet over medium heat.

2. Add carrots and red potatoes. Simmer about 10 minutes.

3. Slice chicken breast into strips and season with lemon pepper and salt.

4. Add chicken to the carrots and potatoes.

5. Stir together and cook, flipping potatoes and carrots often.

6. Cook for 20 minutes until chicken is done.

7. Remove and sprinkle with lemon pepper and paprika.

8. Garnish with parsley and serve.

Easy College Chicken Lunch

Serves: 2

Cooking Time: 30 minutes

Ingredients:

Chicken Breasts, 2

Salt, ½ tsp

Pepper, ½ tsp

Seasoned salt, ½ tsp

Vegetable Oil, ½ cup

Directions:

1. Beat chicken breast on cutting board until flat.

2. Season both sides of chicken with salt, pepper and seasoned salt.

3. Heat oil over medium heat.

4. Place chicken breasts in heated oil.

5. Cook for 15 minutes per side, until chicken is done.

6. Garnish with herbs of choice and serve with side of choice.

Baked 'N' Fried Chicken
Serves: 4

Cooking Time: 40 minutes

Ingredients:

Chicken, 2 large, boneless

Milk, 3 cups

All-purpose flour, 1 cup

Paprika, 1 Tbsp

Seasoned Salt, 1 Tbsp

Pepper, 1 tsp

Butter, ½ stick, melted

Parsley, ½ cup chopped

Directions:

1. Heat oven to 400F and add butter to cast iron skillet.

2. Cut each chicken breast into half. Place chicken in bowl and add milk.

3. Combine flour, paprika, seasoned salt and pepper.

4. Dip each chicken breast in flour mixture and add to cast iron skillet.

5. Bake for 20 minutes, flip chicken, and bake for 20 more minutes.

6. Garnish with parsley.

7. Serve with side of choice.

Bacon, Turkey And Avocado Sandwich

Serves: 2

Cooking Time: 20 minutes

Ingredients:

Turkey, 4 slices

Bacon, 4 slices, cooked

Avocado, peeled and sliced

Butter, 2 Tbsp

Cooking Oil, 1 Tbsp

Bread, 4 slices, any type,

Directions:

1. Heat oil in cast iron skillet over medium heat.

2. Butter 1 side of each slice of bread.

3. Add, turkey, 2 slices of bacon, and slices of avocado.

4. Add other slices of bread.

5. Cook in oil for 10 minutes each side, making sure sides are brown.

6. Remove and serve with any side of preference.

Cast Iron Skillet Steak Sandwich

Serves: 4

Cooking Time: 30 minutes

Ingredients:

Onions, 2, sliced

Canola Oil, 2 Tbsp

Salt, ¼ tsp

Butter, 2 Tbsp

Rib Steak, boneless, cooked and sliced thin

Olive Oil, 2 Tbsp

Salt, to taste

Pepper, to taste

Mozzarella Cheese, 2 cups

Barbeque Sauce, ½ cup

Hoagie Buns, 4, split

Directions:

1. Heat oil in cast iron skillet over medium heat.

2. Pre-cook the onions in oil and set aside.

3. Butter each side of hoagie bun and brown in heated cast iron skillet.

4. Add sliced steak, cheese, onions and barbecue sauce to each hoagie.

5. Place other hoagie on top of barbeque sauce and place in heated oil.

6. Brown on each side for at least 15 minutes until brown and cheese is melted.

7. Serve with side dish of salad or chips.

Flank Steak Sauté
Serves: 4

Cooking Time: 25 Minutes

Ingredients:

Oil, 3 Tbsp

Asparagus, ½ lb., cut diagonally

Flank Steak, 1 lb., cut into thin strips

Red Bell Pepper, 1, cut into strips

Cornstarch, 2 tsp

Water, 3 Tbsp

Sauce:

Soy sauce, 3 Tbsp

Ginger, 1 tsp., finely chopped

Garlic, 1 clove, minced

Green Onion, 1, chopped

Chili Oil, ½ tsp

Directions:

1. Heat oil in cast iron skillet over medium heat.

2. Blend soy sauce, ginger, garlic, green onion and chili oil together to make sauce.

3. Cook asparagus first, for 5 minutes, remove and set aside.

4. Add more oil and cook the steak strips for 5 minutes. Remove and set aside.

5. Add last of oil and cook bell peppers until tender, about 5 minutes.

6. Combine peppers, asparagus and steak in skillet. Add cornstarch dissolved in water.

7. Add sauce and continue frying for 10 minutes

8. Remove and serve with rice on the side.

Burger Ultimate
Serves: 4

Cooking Time: 30 minutes

Ingredients:

Ground Chuck, 1 lb

Venison, 1 lb

Worcestershire Sauce, ½ cup

Garlic Powder, 2 tsp

Seasoned Salt, 2 tsp

Pepper, 1 tsp

Hamburger Buns, 4

Butter, 2 Tbsp

Directions:

1. Combine chuck, venison, Worcestershire sauce, garlic powder, seasoned salt and pepper.

2. Form into 4 large patties.

3. Heat cast iron skillet on medium heat.

4. Melt butter and add buns to brown them. Remove and set aside.

5. Place patties in heated skillet and cook for 30 minutes or until done to each one's preference.

6. Serve on bun, with sliced tomatoes, lettuce, onions and condiment of choice.

7. Side items can be homemade fries or potato chips.

Hamburger Gravy Over Toasted Bread

Serves: 4 to 6

Cooking Time: 45 minutes

Ingredients:

Ground Beef, 1 lb

Beef Stock, 1 can

Flour, 4 Tbsp

Milk, ½ cup

Salt, 1 tsp

Pepper, ¼ tsp

Onion Salt, ¼ tsp

Bread, 6 slices

Directions:

1. Cook ground beef in cast iron skillet and drain.

2. Add flour, salt, pepper, and onion salt and brown.

3. Add beef stock and milk.

4. Cook until gravy becomes thickened.

5. Toast bread and spoon hamburger gravy over toast.

6. Serve warm.

Cast Iron Skillet Thai Basil Beef

Serves: 4

Cooking Time: 20 minutes

Ingredients:

Carrots, 2, cut into matchsticks

Bell peppers, 1, sliced

Hot red pepper, 1, sliced

Green Onions, 2 chopped

Fish Sauce, 1 Tbsp

Honey, ½ tsp

Sesame Oil, 2 Tbsp

Lime, juice of 1

Garlic, 4 cloves, minced

Ginger, 2 tsp, grated

Ground Beef, 1 lb., lean

Pepper, ¼ tsp

Soy Sauce, ⅓ cup plus 2 Tbsp

Thai Sweet Chili Sauce, ⅓ cup

Basil Leaves, 2 cups

Sesame Seeds, ½ cup, toasted

Peanuts, ½ cup chopped and roasted

Directions:

1. Combine carrots, peppers, hot red pepper, green onions, fish sauce, honey, lime juice and 2 Tbsp. of soy sauce. Set aside.

2. Heat oil in cast iron skillet over medium heat.

3. Add garlic and ginger, cook a few seconds and add beef.

4. Season with pepper and brown.

5. Add soy sauce, chili sauce and 1 cup of basil.

6. Simmer and cook until sauce covers the beef.

7. Remove and add remaining basil.

8, Serve with rice. Add beef, then add carrot and pepper mixture on top.

Cast Iron Skillet Beef & Bean Burrito
Serves: 4

Cooking Time: 20 to 30 minutes

Ingredients:

Refried Beans, 1 can, any brand

Ground Beef, 1 lb

Onion, ½ cup, chopped

Chili Powder, ½ tsp

Cumin, ½ tsp

Salt, ¼ tsp

Pepper, ¼ tsp

Flour Tortillas, 4, medium

Directions:

1. Brown ground beef in cast iron skillet and drain.

2. Heat refried beans and add to ground beef.

3. Add onion, chili powder, cumin, salt and pepper and heat.

4. Place mixture in center of tortillas and fold edges in and roll.

5. These can be frozen and heated in microwave.

Beef & Broccoli Skillet

Serves: 4

Cooking Time: 10 minutes

Ingredients:

Chicken Stock, ½ cup

Soy Sauce, ⅔ cup

Rice Vinegar, 2 Tbsp

Honey, ¼ cup

Brown Sugar, 2 Tbsp

Sesame Oil, 1 Tbsp

Garlic, 3 cloves, minced

Cornstarch, 1 Tbsp

Ginger, 1 tsp., ground

Sriracha, 1 tsp

Red Pepper Flakes, ¼ tsp

Water, ¼ cup

Olive Oil, 1 Tbsp

Flank Steak, 1 lb., sliced thin

Broccoli, 1 head, cut in florets

Directions:

1. Combine chicken stock, soy sauce, vinegar, honey, brown sugar, sesame oil, garlic, cornstarch, ginger, Sriracha, red pepper flakes and water.

2. Heat olive oil in cast iron skillet. Cook steak until browned, about 4 minutes.

3. Add soy sauce mix and broccoli. Cook for 6 minutes until sauce is thick.

4. Serve warm.

Cast Iron Skillet Taco Pizza Rolls
Serves: 6

Cooking Time: 15 Minutes

Ingredients:

Ground Beef, ½ oz.

Pizza Crust, 1 can, refrigerated

Taco Seasoning Mix, 2 Tbsp

Water, 3 Tbsp

Mexican Cheese, 1 cup, shredded

Lettuce, tomato, sour cream, onion and guacamole

Directions:

1. Cook ground beef in cast iron skillet over medium heat.

2. Drain. Add taco seasoning, water and Mexican cheese.

3. Roll dough into a rectangle.

4. Add ground beef mixture, top with cheese and roll up.

5. Cut into 1 inch slices.

6. Place slices in large cast iron skillet and bake in 400F preheated oven for 15 minutes.

7. Serve with toppings of choice.

Easy Baked French Dipped Sandwiches
Serves: 2

Cooking Time: 20 minutes

Ingredients:

Sliced Roast Beef, 6, sliced thin

Provolone Cheese, 4 slices

Hoagie Rolls, 2

Butter, 2 Tbsp

Beef Stock, 1 can

Directions:

1. Butter each hoagie roll and brown in cast iron skillet.

2. Add 3 slices of roast beef and 2 slices of provolone cheese to each hoagie.

3. Bake in cast iron skillet at 375F for 20 minutes.

4. Heat beef stock and pour into 2 small bowls for dipping.

5. Quick and easy!

Cast Iron Skillet Pork Burger

Serves: 4

Cooking Time: 30 Minutes

Ingredients:

Ground Pork, 1 lb

Seasoned Salt, 1 Tbsp

Garlic Powder, 1 tsp

Pepper, 1 tsp

Green Onions, 2 chopped

Cooking Oil, 2 Tbsp

Directions:

1. Mix ground pork, seasoned salt, garlic powder, pepper and green onions.

2. Form into patties.

3. Heat oil in cast iron skillet over medium heat.

4. Place patties in heated skillet and cook for 15 minutes on each side until brown.

5. Serve with your choice of toppings and condiments.

Skillet Boneless Pork Chops

Serves: 4

Cooking Time: 30 minutes

Ingredients:

Boneless Pork Chops, 4

Cooking Oil, ½ cup

Flour, 1 cup

Salt, 1 tsp

Pepper, 1 tsp

Seasoned Salt, 1 tsp

Egg, 1

Milk, 1 cup

Directions:

1. Heat oil in cast iron skillet on medium heat.

2. Mix egg and milk, blend well.

3. Mix flour, salt, pepper and seasoned salt together.

4. Dip pork chops in egg mixture and place in flour mixture.

5. Shake and place floured pork chop in heated oil.

6. Cook for 15 minutes on each side until browned.

7. Drain on paper towel.

8. Serve with sides of choice.

Pineapple Teriyaki Pork Chops

Serves: 4

Cooking Time: 30 minutes

Ingredients:

Pineapple Slices, 20 oz. can, save ½ cup juice

Soy Sauce, ⅓ cup

Brown Sugar, 2 Tbsp

Rice Vinegar, 2 Tbsp

Ginger, ½ tsp. ground

Pork Chops, 4, boneless

Chives, 1 tsp., chopped

Directions:

1. Combine soy sauce, brown sugar, rice vinegar, pineapple juice and ginger.

2. Pour in bowl and add pork chops. Marinate for 1 hour.

3. Heat cast iron skillet over medium heat.

4. Add pork chops and cook for 10 minutes on each side, marinate with soy mixture while cooking chops.

5. Remove chops and add sliced pineapples to pan and cook a 5 minutes on each side.

6. Add a pineapple slice to each pork chop and serve.

Cast Iron Skillet Roasted Pork Medallions

Serves: 4

Cooking Time: 30 Minutes

Ingredients:

Cooking Spray

Thyme, 2 tsp

Oregano, 2 tsp

Garlic Powder, 1 tsp

Salt, 1 tsp

Onion Powder, 1 tsp

Pepper, 1 tsp

Olive Oil, 2 tsp

Pork Tenderloin, 2 lb.

Directions:

1. Mix thyme, oregano, garlic powder, salt, onion powder, and pepper.

2. Rub pork tenderloin with mixture.

3. Place olive oil in cast iron skillet and preheat oven to 400F.

4. Place tenderloin in skillet and bake for 30 minutes.

5. When done, slice in medallion size slices.

6. Serve with sides of choice.

Lemon Rosemary Pork Chops

Serves: 4

Cooking Time: 30 minutes

Ingredients:

Garlic, 2 cloves

Kosher Salt, ½ tsp

Lemon Zest, 2 tsp

Rosemary, 2 tsp., chopped

Pork Chops, 4, bone-in

Pepper, 1 tsp

Olive Oil, 1 Tbsp

Lemon Juice, 2 tsp

Dijon Mustard, ½ tsp

Baby Arugula, 4 cups

Pecorino Romano Cheese, ½ cup

Directions:

1. Smash garlic cloves, add salt and make a paste.

2. Mix ¼ tsp. of paste, add lemon zest and rosemary.

3. Rub chops with rosemary paste on both sides.

4. Preheat oven to 375F.

5. Place pork chops in cast iron skillet and place in oven. Cook for 30 minutes.

6. Mix lemon juice, olive oil and Dijon mustard with garlic paste.

7. Pour on arugula and coat well. Sprinkle with cheese.

8. Serve warm.

Bruschetta Pork Chops

Serves: 4

Cooking Time: 20 minutes

Ingredients:

Pork Chops, 4 boneless

Tomatoes, 2 large, diced

Red Onion, ½ large, diced

Garlic, 3 cloves, minced

Olive Oil, 3 Tbsp

Balsamic Vinegar, 1 ½ Tbsp

Salt, ½ tsp

Basil Leaves, cut thin strips

Mozzarella Cheese, 1 cup, shredded

Salt, ¼ tsp

Pepper, ¼ tsp

Directions:

1. Heat cast iron skillet over medium heat. Salt and pepper pork chops. Baste with 2 Tbsp. olive oil.

2. Cook on both sides about 10 minutes each. Mix tomatoes, onion, garlic and 1 Tbsp. olive oil for bruschetta.

3. Spread cheese on top of chops. Broil in cast iron skillet and oven until cheese melts. Spoon bruschetta topping on chops and sprinkle with balsamic vinegar.

Cast Iron Skillet Pork & Ramen Stir-Fry

Serves: 4

Cooking Time: 25 minutes

Ingredients:

Soy Sauce, ¼ cup

Ketchup, 2 Tbsp

Worcestershire Sauce, 2 Tbsp

Sugar, 2 tsp

Red Pepper Flakes, ¼ tsp

Canola Oil, 3 tsp., divided

Pork Chops, 1 lb., cut into small strips

Broccoli Florets, 1 cup

Coleslaw Mix, 4 cups

Bamboo Shoots, 1 can, drained

Garlic, 4 cloves, minced

Ramen Noodles, 2 pkg

Directions:

1. Mix soy sauce, ketchup, Worcestershire sauce, sugar, oil and red pepper flakes. Set aside.

2. Cook pork in heated cast iron skillet until done, about 10 minutes.

3. Add 2 tsp. oil, cook broccoli for 3 minutes. Add coleslaw mix, bamboo shoots and garlic.

Cook for about 7 minutes. Stir in soy sauce mix and pork chops.

4. Cook noodles and drain. Add noodles to the pork mixture in skillet and cook 5 more minutes.

5. Serve warm.

Honey And Soy Pork Chops

Serves: 4

Cooking Time: 15 Minutes

Ingredients:

Pork Chops, 4, thick

Soy Sauce, ¾ cup

Honey, ½ cup

Ginger, Small piece, grated

Garlic, 2 cloves, minced

Chili pepper, 1 small, seeds removed and chopped

Lemon juice, 1 Tbsp

Salad:

Mixed salad greens

Sugar Snap Peas, 1 cup

Dressing:

Olive Oil, 3 Tbsp

Lemon Juice, 3 Tbsp

Salt, ¼ tsp

Pepper, ¼ tsp

Directions:

1. Combine soy sauce, honey, ginger, garlic, chili and lemon juice. Mix well and pour into a large ziplock bag.

2. Place pork chops in bag and marinate 1 to 2 hours.

3. Heat cast iron skillet over high heat. Marinate while chops are cooking.

4. Mix olive oil, lemon juice, salt and pepper. Pour over salad.

5. Lay 1 pork chop on top of 1 serving of salad.

6. Serve and enjoy.

Hot Ham And Cheese
Serves: 2

Cooking Time: 20 minutes

Ingredients:

Ham, 4 slices, deli-style

Cheese, 4 slices, cheese of choice

Butter, 2 Tbsp

Bread, 4 slices

Directions:

1. Heat cast iron skillet over medium heat.

2. Butter the 4 slices of bread.

3. Add two slices of ham and two slices of cheese to two slices of bread.

4. Place the other two slices of bread on top of the cheese.

5. Cook in cast iron skillet for 10 minutes on each side, until browned.

6. Remove, cut in half, and serve.

Cast Iron Shrimp Scampi Quesadillas

Serves: 4

Cooking Time: 15 minutes

Ingredients:

Frozen Shrimp Scampi, 1 box, 12 oz.

Flour Tortillas, 4, 6-inch

Cheddar Cheese, ½ cup, grated

Parmesan Cheese, ⅓ cup

Directions:

1. Heat cast iron skillet over medium heat.

2. Sauté shrimp scampi for 5 minutes, stirring occasionally.

3. Remove shrimp and chop.

4. Place tortilla in heated skillet.

5. Top half of the tortilla with shrimp scampi, cheddar cheese and parmesan cheese.

6. Fold to cover the mixture.

7. Cook for 5 minutes on each side until browned and cheese is melted.

8. Serve with sauce of your choice.

Skillet Salmon Croquette Balls With Dill Sauce

Serves: 6

Cooking Time: 30 minutes

Ingredients:

Salmon, 2 cans, boneless

Potatoes, 1 lb., peeled and boiled

Garlic, 2 cloves, minced

Dill, 1 tsp., chopped

Cilantro, 1 tsp., chopped

Parsley, 1 Tbsp

Chives, 1 Tbsp

Egg Yolks, 3, beaten

Vegetable Oil, 1 cup

Salt, ¼ tsp

Pepper, ¼ tsp

Sauce:

Sour Cream, ⅓ cup

Lemon Juice, 2 Tbsp

Dill, 1 Tbsp

Salt, ¼ tsp

Pepper, ¼ tsp

Directions:

1. Heat oil in cast iron skillet over medium heat.

2. Combine salmon, boiled potatoes, garlic, dill, cilantro, parsley, chives, salt, pepper and egg yolks. Form into balls.

3. Cook in oil for 30 minutes, turning to brown evenly.

4. Drain on paper towel.

5. Serve with dill sauce on the side.

Tuna Quesadillas

Serves: 4

Cooking Time: 10 Minutes

Ingredients:

Vegetable Oil, 3 Tbsp

Tuna, 2 cans, drained

Cream Cheese, 6 oz., softened

Onion, ¼ minced

Garlic Powder, 1 tsp

Salt, 1 tsp

Pepper, 1 tsp

Flour Tortillas, 4, 8- inch

Swiss Cheese, 4 slices

Directions:

1. Heat oil in cast iron skillet over high heat.

2. Mix tuna, cream cheese, onion, garlic powder, salt, pepper and Swiss cheese.

3. Spread tuna mixture on one side of each tortilla. Fold to cover.

4. Cook for 5 minutes on each side until cheese is melted and quesadillas are golden brown.

5. Serve with sauce of choice.

Cast Iron Skillet Salmon Burger

Serves: 2

Cooking Time: 20 minutes

Ingredients:

Vegetable Oil, 1 cup

Tuna, 1 can, drained

Cornmeal, ¼ cup

Egg, 1

Seasoned Salt, 1 Tbsp

Salt, ¼ tsp

Pepper, ¼ tsp

Garlic Powder, ½ tsp

Green Onion, 1 chopped

Buns, 2

Directions:

1. Heat oil in cast iron skillet over medium heat.

2. Mix tuna, cornmeal, egg, seasoned salt, salt, pepper, garlic powder and green onion.

3. Form patties and place in heated oil.

4. Cook for 10 minutes on each side until browned.

5. Place on buns and garnish toppings of your choice. Serve with sides of your choice.

Drained Tuna Melt
Serves: 2

Cooking Time: 20 minutes

Ingredients:

Oil, ½ cup

Tuna, 1 can, drained

Cream Cheese, 1 Tbsp

Salt, ¼ tsp

Pepper, ¼ tsp

Onion Powder, ¼ tsp

Rye Bread, 4 slices

Cheddar Cheese, ¼ cup shredded

Green Onions, 1 chopped

Directions:

1. Heat oil in cast iron skillet over medium heat.

2. Mix tuna, cream cheese, salt, pepper and onion powder.

3. Spread rye bread with mixture. Top with cheese and green onions. Place other 2 slices of rye bread on top of spread and cheese.

4. Cook in skillet for 10 minutes on each side until golden brown and cheese is melted.

5. Serve with soup or salad.

Cast Iron Skillet Fish Tacos

Serves: 6

Cooking Time: 10 minutes

Ingredients:

Snapper fillets, 2 lbs.

Salt, ¼ tsp

Pepper, ¼ tsp

Paprika, 2 tsp

Cayenne Pepper, ½ tsp

Garlic Powder, 1 tsp

Cumin, 1 tsp

Canola Oil, 2 Tbsp

Cole Slaw Mix

Mayonnaise, 1 cup

Sugar, 2 tsp

Vinegar, 2 tsp

Sour Cream, ¼ cup

Lime Juice, 1 tsp.

Tortillas, 6, warmed

Directions:

1. Mix salt, pepper, paprika, cayenne, garlic powder and cumin.

2. Season fish on both sides.

3. Heat oil in cast iron skillet over medium heat.

4. Cook fish for 10 minutes, flipping often, until browned.

5. Mix coleslaw mix with mayonnaise, sugar, vinegar, sour cream and lime juice.

6. Cut fish into strips and place on each warm tortilla.

7. Top with coleslaw mix.

8. Serve warm.

Cast Iron Skillet Fish And Chips
Serves: 2

Cooking Time: 20 Minutes

Ingredients:

Potatoes, 4 medium

Fish Fillets, 4 medium

Flour, ½ cup plus 2 Tbsp

Cornstarch, 2 Tbsp

Paprika, ¼ tsp

Onion Powder, ¼ tsp

Vegetable Oil, 1 cup

Directions:

1. Heat oil in cast iron skillet over medium heat.

2. Mix flour, cornstarch, paprika and onion powder.

3. Dip fish and coat on both sides.

4. Slice potatoes into 1-inch strips.

5. Fry potatoes until crisp. Drain on paper towel and set aside.

6. Fry fish until browned and done in the middle.

7. Drain fish and serve with fries.

8. Condiment of choice can be used as a side.

Beer Battered Fish And Potato Wedges

Serves: 4

Cooking Time: 30 minutes

Ingredients:

Oil, 2 cups

Cod Fillets, 1 lb.

Flour, 2 cups

Onion Powder, 1 tsp

Salt, ½ tsp

Pepper, ½ tsp

Beer, 10 oz

Potatoes, 3 large, cut into wedges

Mayonnaise, 1 cup

Pickle, 1 large, chopped

Lemon Juice, ¼ cup

Directions:

1. Mix 1 cup of flour, salt and pepper, set aside.

2. Mix the second cup of flour with onion powder, salt and pepper. Add the beer to this mixture.

3. Heat oil in cast iron skillet over medium heat.

4. Cook potatoes until crispy. Remove and drain on paper towel.

5. Dip fish in flour & beer mixture. Dip in other flour mixture.

6. Cook in heated oil for 10 minutes on each side until browned.

7. Mix mayonnaise, pickle, and lemon juice for tartar sauce.

8. Serve fish with potato wedges and tartar sauce.

Cast Iron Skillet Fried Clams
Serves: 4

Cooking Time: 20 minutes

Ingredients:

Milk, 2 cups

Seafood Seasoning, 2 Tbsp

Lemons, zest of 2

Kosher Salt, 1 tsp

Pepper, 1 tsp

Soft-shelled clams, 10 oz. shucked

Cornmeal, 1 cup

All-Purpose Flour, 1 cup

Vegetable Oil, 1 cup

Directions:

1. Combine milk, 1 Tbsp. of seafood seasoning, lemon zest, ½ tsp. salt, and ½ tsp. pepper. Mix and add clams. Refrigerate until ready to cook, about an hour.

2. Mix cornmeal, flour, ½ tsp seafood seasoning, ½ tsp. salt and ½ tsp. pepper.

3. Heat oil in cast iron skillet over high heat.

4. Lift clams from milk and add to cornmeal mixture. Coat well.

5. Add clams to heated oil and cook for 15 to 20 minutes until browned. Drain on paper towel.

6. Serve with lemon wedges and cocktail sauce.

Pan Seared Scallops

Serves: 4

Cooking Time: 10 minutes

Ingredients:

Sea Scallops, 2 lbs.

Butter, 1 stick

Olive Oil, 2 Tbsp

Salt, ¼ tsp

Pepper, ¼ tsp

Lemon juice, 1 Tbsp

Directions:

1. Heat butter and olive oil in cast iron skillet over high heat.

2. Season scallops with salt and pepper.

3. Add scallops and sear for 5 minutes on each side, spooning butter and oil over top.

4. Do not let the scallops burn.

5. Remove and drain on paper towel.

6. Sprinkle with lemon juice and serve with side of choice.

Beef Hot Dog Stir Fry

Serves: 2

Cooking Time: 20 minutes

Ingredients:

Beef Hot Dogs, 1 pkg. of 8

Onion, 1 small, peeled and sliced into strips

Green Bell Peppers, 1 small, sliced into strips

Coarse Ground Pepper, 1 Tbsp

Kosher Salt, 1 tsp

Olive Oil, 1 Tbsp

Directions:

1. Slice hot dogs at a slant into 1-inch pieces.

2. Heat olive oil in cast iron skillet over medium heat.

3. Add hot dog slices, pepper, salt, bell pepper and onions.

4. Stir fry for 10 minutes until vegetables are tender.

5. Remove and serve over rice.

Cast Iron Skillet Kielbasa

Serves: 4

Cooking Time: 20 minutes

Ingredients:

Kielbasa, 1 lb. pkg.

Onions, 1 small, sliced in strips

Salt, 1 tsp

Pepper, 1 tsp

Vegetable Oil, 1 Tbsp

Rosemary, ¼ cup

Directions:

1. Heat oil in cast iron skillet over medium heat.

2. Add slice onions, salt and pepper.

3. Sauté onions, then add Kielbasa.

4. Cook for 20 minutes, turning often until evenly browned.

5. Sprinkle with rosemary and serve.

Italian Grilled Cheese

Serves: 1

Cooking Time: 10 minutes

Ingredients:

Ciabatta Bread, 2 slices

Mozzarella Cheese, 1 slice

Butter, 1 Tbsp

Spicy Salami, 1 slice

Red Bell Pepper, 1 slice

Pasta Sauce, for dipping

Italian Olive Antipasto, 1 Tbsp

Directions:

1. Heat butter in cast iron skillet.

2. Spread ciabatta bread with antipasto.

3. Add mozzarella cheese, salami and bell pepper.

4. Cook in butter for 5 minutes on each side until cheese is melted and bread is toasted.

5. Serve with pasta sauce for dipping.

Skillet Hawaiian Grilled Cheese

Serves: 1

Cooking Time: 10 minutes

Ingredients:

Bread, 2 slices of your choice

Pineapple, canned, 3 slices

Canadian Bacon, 3 slices

Monterey Jack Cheese, 2 slices

Butter, 1 Tbsp

Oregano, ¼ tsp

Parsley, ¼ tsp

Directions:

1. Melt butter in cast iron skillet.

2. Layer bread with pineapple slices, bacon, oregano, parsley and cheese.

3. Add sandwich to heated butter and cook on each side for 5 minutes or until bread is toasted and bread is toasted.

4. Remove, slice and serve with side of choice.

Cast Iron Skillet Barbecued Grilled Cheese

Serves: 4

Cooking Time: 15 minutes

Ingredients:

Challah Bread, 8 slices

Sharp Cheddar Cheese, 4 slices

Pepper Jack Cheese, 4 slices

Onion, 1 large, sliced thin

Butter, 3 Tbsp

BBQ sauce, 4 Tbsp

Directions:

1. Melt butter in cast iron skillet.

2. Make sandwiches with bread, cheddar cheese, pepper jack cheese, onion and BBQ sauce.

3. Add sandwich to heated butter and cook for 5 minutes on each side until browned and cheese is melted.

4. Slice and serve with side of choice.

Clubhouse Grill In Skillet

Serves: 1

Cooking Time: 10 minutes

Ingredients:

Texas Toast, 2 slices

Butter, 1 Tbsp

Mayonnaise, 2 tsp

Cheddar Cheese, 1 slice

Jack Cheese, 1 slice

Ham, 3 slices

Turkey Breast, 3 slices

Bacon, 2 slices, thick sliced, cooked crispy

Tomato, 2 slices

Honey BBQ Sauce, 2 tsp.

Lettuce, ¼ cup, shredded

Directions:

1. Melt butter in cast iron skillet.

2. Spread each slice of Texas Toast with mayonnaise.

3. Add cheddar cheese, jack cheese, ham, turkey breast, bacon, tomato, bbq sauce and lettuce.

4. Cook in heated butter for 5 minutes on each side or until bread is toasted and cheese is melted. Remove and cut into 4 sections. Serve with side of choice.

Cast Iron Skillet Grilled Cheese

Serves: 1

Cooking Time: 10 minutes

Ingredients:

Bread, 2 slices, any type

Cheddar Cheese, 2 slices

Butter, 1 Tbsp

Directions:

1. Heat butter in skillet over medium heat.

2. Spread each bread slice with butter.

3. Add cheese and make sandwich.

4. Cook in heated butter for 5 minutes on each side until bread is toasted and cheese is melted.

5. Remove, cut in half, and serve with side of choice.

Cast Iron Skillet Pepperoni Pizza
Serves: 2

Cooking Time: 20 minutes:

Ingredients:

Pizza Dough, 1 pkg. prepared

Pizza Sauce, 1 jar

Mozzarella Cheese, 1 cup, shredded

Pepperoni, 1 pkg

Oil, 1 Tbsp

Directions:

1. Preheat cast iron skillet in 400F oven.

2. Grease skillet and press in dough.

3. Add pizza sauce, mozzarella cheese and pepperoni.

4. Bake for 20 minutes until the edges are brown.

5. Remove, slice and serve.

Feta Flatbread Savor
Serves: 4

Cooking Time: 20 minutes

Ingredients:

Olive Oil, 4 Tbsp

Water, ½ cup

Egg, 1 scrambled

All-purpose Flour, ½ cup plus 2 Tbsp

Salt, ¼ tsp

Baking Powder, ¼ tsp

Feta Cheese, 5 oz., crumbled

Butter, 1 Tbsp., softened

Directions:

1. Preheat oven to 450F with cast iron skillet inside.

2. Combine water, 2 Tbsp. olive oil, and egg.

3. Combine flour, baking powder and salt.

4. Mix water mixture and flour mixture.

5. Remove pan and wipe with remaining olive oil

6. Pour mixture into pan and sprinkle feta cheese on top.

7. Dab butter on top of feta cheese.

8. Bake for 20 minutes or until crust is browned. Remove, slice and serve.

Prosciutto Pizza With Mushroom & Leek

Serves: 4

Cooking Time: 20 minutes

Ingredients:

Butter, 1 Tbsp

Leek, 1 large, diced

Mushrooms, 2 cups, sliced

Salt, ¼ tsp

Pepper, ¼ tsp

Olive Oil, 2 tsp

Pizza Dough, 1 pkg., thawed

Mozzarella Cheese, 2 cups, grated

Prosciutto, 4 slices

Directions:

1. Melt butter in cast iron skillet, sauté leeks until tender.

2. Add mushrooms and sauté. Add salt and pepper.

3. Grease cast iron skillet with oil and press pizza dough in skillet.

4. Spread leek mixture over pizza dough.

5. Spread cheese over top.

6. Bake in 450F preheated oven for 20 minutes.

7. Spread prosciutto over top. Slice and serve.

Vegetable Pizza

Serves: 4

Cooking Time: 20 minutes

Ingredients:

Cauliflower, 2 cups, shredded

Egg, 1 large

Garlic Powder, ¼ tsp

Italian Seasoning, 1 tsp

Mozzarella Cheese, 2 cups, shredded

Pizza Sauce, ¼ cup

Mushrooms, ½ cup sliced

Onions, ¼ cup

Black Olives, 1 small can

Parmesan Cheese, 1 Tbsp

Directions:

1. Microwave cauliflower for 8 minutes.

2. Remove and add egg, cheese, garlic powder and Italian seasoning.

3. Put crust in cast iron skillet sprayed with cooking spray.

4. Spray cooking spray on crust.

5. Add sauce, mushrooms, onions and black olives. Spread mozzarella on top.

6. Bake in 400F preheated oven and cook for 20 minutes.

7. Remove and sprinkle parmesan cheese on top.

8. Slice and serve.

Cast Iron Skillet Nachos

Serves: 2

Cooking Time: 10 minutes

Ingredients:

Black Beans, 1 can, drained

Ground Beef, 1 lb., cooked and drained

Minced Onion, 1 tsp

Taco Seasoning, 1 tsp

Tortilla Chips, 1 bag

Green Bell Pepper, 1, chopped

Tomato, 1 medium, chopped

Queso Cheese Sauce, 1 jar

Cheddar Cheese, 1 cup, shredded

Directions:

1. Brown hamburger and drain. Add bell pepper, onion and taco seasoning and mix.

2. Place tortilla chips in cast iron skillet. Sprinkle half of ground beef mixture over chips.

3. Add black beans and sprinkle with cheese. Pour queso over the mix.

4. Repeat layers of chips, ground beef, black beans, cheese and queso.

5. Bake in 350F preheated oven for 10 minutes. Remove and sprinkle with bell peppers and tomatoes.

Bacon Spicy Cheese Fries

Serves: 2

Cooking Time: 40 minutes

Ingredients:

Cooking Spray

Cornstarch, 2 Tbsp

Chili Powder, 2 tsp

Chipotle Chili Powder, 1 tsp

Paprika, ½ tsp

Cumin, ¼ tsp

Salt, ¼ tsp

Potatoes, 2 large

Olive Oil, 2 Tbsp

Worcestershire Sauce, 1 tsp

Cheddar Cheese, ¾ cup

Chives, 2 Tbsp

Bacon, 6 slices, cooked and crumbled

Directions:

1. Combine cornstarch, chili powder, chipotle chili powder, paprika, cumin and salt.

2. Peel potatoes and cut into wedges.

3. Mix Worcestershire sauce, seasoned salt and olive oil.

4. Coat potatoes in Worcestershire sauce mixture.

5. Spread potatoes with cornstarch mixture. Coat well.

6. Spray cast iron skillet with cooking spray.

7. Cook in 425F preheated oven for 40 minutes, stirring to evenly cook.

8. Spread cheese over potatoes and place back in oven to melt cheese.

9. Remove and sprinkle with chives and bacon.

10. Serve warm.

Cast Iron Skillet Fried Eggplant

Serves: 4

Cooking Time: 30 minutes

Ingredients:

Eggplant, 1 large, fresh

Eggs, 6

Water, 1 Tbsp

Italian Bread Crumbs, 3 to 4 cups

Cooking Oil, 1 cup

Directions:

1. Heat oil in cast iron skillet over medium heat.

2. Combine eggs and water. Mix well.

3. Slice eggplant in ½ inch thick slices.

4. Dip eggplant in egg mixture, then in bread crumbs.

5. Fry in cast iron skillet for 15 minutes on each side until golden brown.

6. Drain and serve with side of choice.

BOOK 3

CAST IRON SKILLET COOKBOOK: VOL.3 Dinner RECIPES

Introduction

Imagine great flavor and family time all tied into one! This is what you will get with cast iron skillet dinners. The cast iron skillet has been around for generations. Mothers hand the skillets down to their daughters along with the recipes that have delighted for years. Some of the recipes are old traditions, while some of the recipes are new and innovative. Make some new family recipes in your cast iron skillet.

Be sure to season your skillet. The seasoning of your skillet can be the key to wonderful tasting meats and vegetables. Keep your skillets oiled to prevent rusting. Do not be scared of cast iron. It is a versatile cooking tool which can be used to fry, bake, sear and Sauté. Heat is held longer in a cast iron skillet, which will cook your foods evenly. They are durable and flexible as well. Simple dishes can be cooked or exotic cuisines can be created. They are not limited to the classic dishes.

Make a mean skillet of spaghetti or a Chinese delicacy. Any ethnic meal you want to cook is great in a cast iron skillet. You are able to fry tasty fried chicken, Sauté onions and peppers, bake a beautiful skillet of cornbread or bake a roast. Any of these dishes are delicious and will make you want to try different recipes. Make a one dish meal that will delight the pickiest of eaters.

Cast iron skillets can be used in the home and at the campground. It can withstand the high temperatures of an open pit. This will make camping feel something like home. Frying is a great activity in a cast iron skillet—it was made for this. Since they are durable, they will last for many years to come. So get your skillet, get it seasoned and get to cooking.

Years of recipes are waiting for you to cook. Check your cabinet content and spices to make sure there are several ingredients. Some of the most basic ingredients can create a tasty dish. Meats and vegetables are always good to combine for the family dinner. If you are not a meat lover, plenty of meatless dishes can be created. Whatever your preference is whatever makes your stomach happy and full.

The cast iron skillet can withstand metal spatulas, wooden spoons, forks and spoons. It will not scratch. It can always be re-seasoned and oiled to be ready to use again. It is a good idea to have two or more skillets, cooking cake in a skillet seasoned for meat may make the taste of cake different. You need one for cooking meats and vegetables and one for cooking desserts.

The older skillets are heavier than the newer skillets. The newer skillets are a little lighter in weight. They can also be purchased pre-seasoned. When you season a skillet, you are actually baking oil into the pores of the skillet. You can clean specks of food off the skillet by using coarse salt. If you are camping out, sand will clean the food specks off. You then just wipe out after the food specks are gone.

The cast iron cooking ware goes back at least 200 years. Before the cooking range was invented, the only source to cook with was the fireplace. There were skillets, pots and pans. They withstood the heat and proved to be a source of cookware that could cook anything. Non-sticking can be achieved with the cast iron skillet. The more it is seasoned and used, the less it will stick. Making an omelet will be easy. Meat will not stick; potatoes will come out fried perfect.

Cast iron is perfect for fried or scrambled eggs, golden brown pancakes, crepes or even baking cakes. The temperature is even and hot. It is a wonderful addition to your kitchen. Make perfect cornbread to eat with the delectable meats and vegetables. Dinner is the family time meal. Get the husband and kids together and share wonderful meals with them. Grab a couple of skillets and get to cooking. Your family will appreciate the ingenious way you create meals.

Respect your cast iron skillet and use it often. Your cast iron skillet will serve you well for many years. Be sure to clean after each use, do not let it soak or stay wet, season and oil it as needed. Store your skillet properly. Do not place in an area where rust can build up. If this happens, re-oil and bake for a couple of hours. The skillet should be good as new.

However you get your skillet, whether bought or handed down, treat it well. Cook often and create wonderful meals. The cast iron skillet will become your valued friend in the kitchen.

Don't be afraid to try. Get it out and get started!

CAST IRON SKILLET DINNER RECIPES

Cast Iron Skillet Chicken Casserole

Serves: 6

Cooking Time: 15 minutes

Ingredients:

Cooking Spray

Chicken, 3 cups cooked

Cream of Chicken Soup, 1 can

Celery, 1 cup chopped

Onion, 2 tsp., minced

Pepper, ¼ tsp

Salt, ½ tsp

Eggs, 3 hard cooked, sliced

Lemon Juice, 1 Tbsp

Mayonnaise, ¾ cup

Almonds, ½ cup

Directions:

1. Spray cast iron skillet with cooking spray.

2. Mix all ingredients, except almonds, and pour in skillet.

3. Bake in 450F preheated oven for 15 minutes.

4. Remove and sprinkle with almonds.

5. Serve with warm bread and butter.

Chicken Almondine

Serves: 4

Cooking Time: 25 minutes

Ingredients:

Chicken, 3 cups, cooked

Cream of chicken soup, 1 can

Water Chestnuts, 1 can, drained and sliced

Mushrooms, 1 can, drained

Mayonnaise, ⅔ cup

Celery, ½ cup

Sour Cream, ½ cup

Onion, ½ cup, chopped

Crescent Rolls, 1 can

Swiss Cheese, ⅔ cup, shredded

Slivered Almonds, ½ cup

Butter, 4 Tbsp., melted

Directions:

1. Mix chicken, soup, water chestnuts, mushrooms, mayonnaise, celery, sour cream and onions.

2. Pour into cast iron skillet.

3. Separate crescent rolls into 2 long triangles.

4. Place dough over chicken.

5. Combine rest of ingredients and pour over chicken.

6. Bake in 375F preheated oven for 25 minutes.

7. Remove and enjoy!

Stir-Fry Chicken

Serves: 4

Cooking Time: 20 minutes

Ingredients:

Oil, 2 Tbsp

Broccoli, 1 cup

Cauliflower, 1 cup

Carrot Strips, ¾ cup

Green Onions, ¼ cup

Garlic, 1 clove, minced

Chicken Breasts, 3 cut into bite size pieces

Salad Dressing, ½ cup

Soy Sauce, 1 Tbsp

Ginger, ½ tsp

Directions:

1. Heat 1 Tbsp. oil in cast iron skillet over medium heat.

2. Stir-fry the vegetables and garlic for 5 to 10 minutes. Remove vegetables.

3. Add rest of oil and cook chicken for 5 minutes. Add vegetables to cooked chicken.

4. Combine salad dressing, soy sauce and ginger. Add to chicken and vegetables.

5. Heat another 5 to 10 minutes until heated through. Serve with rice.

Cast Iron Skillet Chicken Alfredo

Serves: 4

Cooking Time: 25 minutes

Ingredients:

Olive Oil, 3 Tbsp

Chicken Breast, 1 ½ lb. boneless and skinless

Garlic, 2 cloves, minced

Chicken Broth, 1 can

Heavy Cream, 1 cup

Penne Pasta, ½ lb., uncooked

Parmesan Cheese, 2 cups

Salt, ¼ tsp

Pepper, ¼ tsp

Parsley, for garnish

Directions:

1. Dice chicken breasts, season with salt and pepper.

2. Heat olive oil in cast iron skillet and brown chicken.

3. Add garlic, chicken broth, cream and pasta to pan and combine.

4. Bring to boil, reduce and simmer for 25 minutes.

5. Remove and add parmesan cheese.

6. Garnish with parsley and serve.

Cast Iron Skillet Lemon Garlic Chicken Pasta

Serves: 4

Cooking Time: 25 minutes

Ingredients:

Olive Oil, ¼ cup

Chicken Breasts, 1 lb., boneless

Salt, 1 tsp

Pepper, 1 tsp

Garlic, 4 cloves minced

Chicken Broth, 2 cups

Water, 1 cup

Pasta, ½ lb

Lemon Juice, ¼ cup

Parmesan Cheese, 1 cup

Basil leaves, 1 cup

Directions:

1. Cut chicken into chunks and season with salt and pepper.

2. Heat oil in skillet over medium heat.

3. Brown chicken breasts and add garlic. Combine.

4. Add chicken broth, water and pasta.

5. Cook to boiling, reduce heat and simmer for about 25 minutes.

6. Remove, stir in lemon juice and parmesan cheese.

7. Garnish with basil and serve.

Cast Iron Skillet Chicken Drumsticks & Potatoes

Serves: 4

Cooking Time: 1 hour, 15 minutes

Ingredients:

Drumsticks, 8

Potatoes, 6 large, cut into quarters

Carrots, 4, cut into small pieces

Salt, 1 tsp

Pepper, 1 tsp

Olive Oil, 4 Tbsp

Directions:

1. Preheat oven to 375F.

2. Pour olive oil in cast iron skillet along with drumsticks, carrots, salt and pepper.

3. Mix to coat evenly.

4. Bake for 1 hour, 15 minutes until potatoes and carrots are tender and chicken is browned.

5. Serve 2 chicken drumsticks with potatoes and carrots per serving.

Catalina Chicken

Serves: 4

Cooking Time: 45 minutes

Ingredients:

Cooking Spray

Chicken, 1 lb., chopped

Chicken Bouillon Granules, 1 pkg

Catalina Dressing, 1 bottle.

Directions:

1. Skin chicken pieces.

2. Arrange in sprayed cast iron skillet.

3. Sprinkle granules over chicken.

4. Pour dressing over the chicken.

5. Cook uncovered for 45 minutes at 350F.

6. Serve with side dish of choice.

Swiss Chicken Casserole

Serves: 4

Cooking Time: 50 minutes

Ingredients:

Oil, 1 Tbsp

Chicken Breasts, 6

Swiss Cheese, 6 slices

Milk, ¼ cup

Cream of Chicken Soup, 1 can

Stuffing Mix, 2 cups

Butter, ¼ stick

Directions:

1. Arrange chicken breasts in lightly greased cast iron skillet.

2. Top with Swiss cheese slices.

3. Combine milk and soup, stir well, and pour over chicken and cheese.

4. Spread stuffing over chicken.

5. Add butter on top of stuffing.

6. Cover and bake at 350F for 50 minutes.

7. Serve with side of choice.

Apricot Glazed Walnut Stuffed Chicken Breast With Potatoes

Serves: 4

Cooking Time: 60 minutes

Ingredients:

Red Potatoes, 1 ½ lb., halved

Olive Oil, 4 Tbsp

Seasoned Salt, 1 ½ tsp

Garlic, 3 cloves, minced

Lemon, zest of 1

Chicken Breasts, 4 boneless with skin on

Walnuts, ½ cup

Basil, 1 cup

Brie Cheese, 6 oz., cubed

Cream Cheese, 2 oz

Egg, 1

Salt, ½ tsp

Pepper, ½ tsp

Red Pepper, ¼ tsp

Apricot Preserves, ¾ cup

Balsamic Vinegar, 1 Tbsp

Directions:

1. Heat olive oil in cast iron skillet in oven preheated to 400F.

2. Add potatoes and coat with 3 Tbsp. olive oil.

3. Season with seasoned salt, pepper and lemon zest.

4. Bake for about 10 minutes.

5. Combine walnuts, basil, garlic, brie, cream cheese and egg. Pulse in blender or food processor to make a paste.

6. Place a spoonful of paste under the chicken skin.

7. Combine 1 Tbsp. olive oil, apricot preserves and balsamic vinegar. Brush chicken breasts with this mixture.

8. Remove potatoes and add chicken breasts to cast iron skillet.

9. Bake for 50 minutes until potatoes and chicken is done.

10. Remove and serve.

Cast Iron Skillet Chicken Cordon Bleu

Serves: 6

Cooking Time: 25 minutes

Ingredients:

Breast Fillets, 6 small

Salt, ¼ tsp

Pepper, ¼ tsp

Panko Bread Crumbs, 1 cup

Parmesan Cheese, ¼ cup

Olive Oil, 4 Tbsp

Deli Ham, 6 slices

Swiss Cheese, 6 slices

Chicken Broth, ½ cup

Parsley, for garnish

Directions:

1. Heat olive oil in cast iron skillet over medium heat.

2. Season breast fillets with salt and pepper.

3. Mix bread crumbs and parmesan cheese.

4. Bread chicken breasts with mixture.

5. Add chicken to heated oil and cook 4 minutes on each side until done.

6. Top each chicken breast with ham and cheese.

7. Pour chicken broth on top and cover. Cook for 3 to 4 minutes until cheese is melted.

8. Serve with rice, salad or pasta.

Bourbon Spiced Chicken Wings
Serves: 10

Cooking Time: 60 minutes

Ingredients:

Chicken Wings, 4 lbs. fresh

Brown Sugar, ½ cup

Paprika, ¼ cup

Salt, 1 tsp

Pepper, 1 tsp

Coriander, 2 tsp

Garlic Powder, 2 tsp

Onion Powder, 2 tsp

Cayenne Pepper, ½ tsp

Basil, 1 tsp

Celery Salt, 1 tsp

Bourbon, 1 cup

Onion, 1 cup, chopped

Water, ½ cup

Ketchup, 1 ½ cups

Tomato Paste, 1 Tbsp

Balsamic Vinegar, 2 Tbsp

Molasses, 4 Tbsp

Worcestershire Sauce, ¼ cup

Liquid Smoke, ¼ tsp

Hot Sauce, ¼ tsp

Directions:

1. Combine brown sugar, paprika, salt, coriander, garlic powder, onion powder, cayenne pepper, basil and celery salt.

2. Add chicken wings and coat well. Marinate overnight.

3. Mix bourbon, onion, water, ketchup, tomato paste, ¼ tsp. brown sugar, vinegar, molasses, Worcestershire sauce, liquid smoke and hot sauce.

4. Spray large cast iron skillets, add chicken wings. Pour barbeque sauce over wings.

5. Cook in 375F preheated oven for 1 hour or until wings are done.

6. Remove and serve with side of coleslaw.

Pecan Crusted Chicken

Serves: 6

Cooking Time: 30 minutes

Ingredients:

Pecan, 1 cup pieces

Salt, 1 tsp

Pepper, ½ tsp

Garlic Powder, ½ tsp

Cayenne Pepper, ¼ tsp

Flour, 1 cup

Water, 3 tsp

Eggs, 2

Chicken Breast Tenders, 1 lb., skinless

Cooking Spray

<u>Directions:</u>

1. Heat oven at 375F.

2. Mix pecan, salt, pepper, garlic powder, cayenne pepper and flour. Crush and mix well.

3. Combine eggs and water, mix well.

4. Dip chicken in egg mixture then in flour mixture. Coat evenly.

5. Spray cast iron skillet with cooking spray.

6. Bake chicken for 30 minutes, turning half way through to cook evenly,

7. Remove and serve with sides of your choice.

Cast Iron Skillet Southwestern Fiesta Rice

Serves: 4

Cooking Time: 25 minutes

Ingredients:

Long grain white rice, 1 cup

Water, 2 cups

Salt, 1 tsp

Lime Juice, ¼ cup

Cilantro, 3 Tbs., chopped

Chicken Breasts, 1 lb., boneless and skinless

Taco Seasoning, 1 pack

Olive Oil, 2 Tbsp

Onion, 2 Tbsp., diced

Bell Pepper, 2 cups, diced

Corn, 2 cups

Garlic, 3 cloves, minced

Black Beans, 1 can, drained

Tomatoes and green chiles, 1 can, drained

Avocado, 1, diced

Directions:

1. Combine rice, water, salt, lime juice, and cilantro. Bring to boil then reduce heat and simmer for 14 minutes.

2. Cut chickens into chunks. Season with taco seasoning.

3. Heat oil in cast iron skillet over medium heat. Cook chicken for 10 minutes until browned.

4. Remove chicken and add onion, bell pepper, corn and rest of taco seasoning. Cook until veggies are blackened. Turn heat down and add garlic. Cook about 1 minute.

5. Add black beans, tomatoes and green chilies and rice. Stir to mix.

6. Garnish with cilantro and avocados.

7. Serve with warm tortillas.

Cast Iron Skillet Peanut Fried Chicken

Serves: 4

Cooking Time: 20 minutes

Ingredients:

Chicken Thighs, 8 boneless, skinless

Peanut Butter, ½ cup

Flour, ½ cup

Salt, ¼ tsp

Red Pepper, ¼ tsp

Peanut Oil, ¼ cup

Directions:

1. Heat peanut oil in cast iron skillet over medium heat.

2. Combine peanut butter, flour, salt and red pepper. Mix well.

3. Rinse chicken thighs and dry.

4. Dip chicken thighs in peanut butter mixture and place in heated oil.

5. Cook for 10 minutes on each side.

6. Remove and let drain on rack.

7. Serve with side dish of choice.

Cast Iron Skillet Whole Roasted Chicken

Serves: 4

Cooking Time: 1 hour

Ingredients:

Chicken, 1 medium Roaster

Butter, ½ stick

Seasoned Salt, 1 tsp

Pepper, 1 tsp

Yukon Gold Potatoes, 1 small Bag

Olive Oil, ¼ cup

Directions:

1. Preheat oven to 450F.

2. Clean potatoes and rub with olive oil. Place in cast iron skillet around the outside edges.

3. Rinse chicken, pat dry and butter.

4. Combine seasoned salt and pepper.

5. Rub chicken with seasoned mixture. Place chicken in middle of potatoes.

6. Cook in cast iron skillet for 1 hour or until done and golden brown.

7. Remove when done and serve with the potatoes.

Pan Roasted Chicken With Bacon & Apples

Serves: 4

Cooking Time: 50 minutes

Ingredients:

Chicken Thighs, 6 large

Salt, 1 tsp

Pepper, ¼ tsp

Broth, 1 cup

Thyme, 4 sprigs

Bacon, ½ pound cooked and crumbled

Green Onions, 1 cup, sliced

Apple, 1 cored and sliced

Directions:

1. Heat cast iron skillet over medium heat.

2. Season chicken thighs with salt and pepper.

3. Add to hot skillet and sear both sides, about 10 minutes.

4. Add broth and thyme.

5. Move to oven heated at 425F and cook for 20 minutes.

6. Brown bacon and drain.

7. Sauté green onions and apples in bacon grease for 5 minutes. Remove and add bacon to mixture.

8. Remove chicken from oven and add bacon mixture in between the chicken thighs. Bake for 15 minutes longer.

9. Remove from oven and serve.

Skillet Chicken Parmesan

Serves: 4

Cooking Time: 15 minutes

Ingredients:

Chicken Cutlets, 4

Olive Oil, 2 tsp

Salt, ½ tsp

Pepper, ¼ tsp

Panko Bread Crumbs, ½ cup

Garlic Powder, ¼ tsp

Oregano, ½ tsp

Basil, ½ tsp

Egg White, 1

Water, 1 tsp

Parmesan Cheese, ¼ cup, divided

Mozzarella Cheese, ½ cup

Marinara Sauce, 1 Jar

Directions:

1. Mix bread crumbs, garlic powder, oregano, basil and 2 Tbsp. of parmesan cheese.

2. Mix egg white and ½ tsp. of water. Mix well.

3. Rub chicken with salt and pepper.

4. Heat olive oil in cast iron skillet over medium heat.

5. Dip chicken into egg mixture, then in the bread crumb mixture. Add to hot oil and cook 5 minutes until browned and done.

6. Set chicken aside. Add marinara sauce and cook for 3 minutes.

7. Put chicken on top of sauce, top with mozzarella cheese.

8. Bake in oven until cheese is melted.

9. Remove and sprinkle with rest of parmesan cheese.

Cast Iron Skillet Chicken & Zucchini

Serves: 6

Cooking Time: 20 minutes

Ingredients:

Olive Oil, 1 Tbsp

Onion, 1 large, chopped

Garlic, 3 cloves, minced

Bell Peppers, 2 medium, chopped

Chicken Breast, 1 lb. boneless and skinless, diced

Cumin, 1 Tbsp

Salt, 1 tsp

Pepper, 1 tsp

Corn, 1 cup

Black Beans, 1 can, drained

Tomatoes, 1 can, diced

Taco Seasoning, 1 tsp

Zucchini, 1 large, diced

Colby Cheese, 1 cup, shredded

Green Onions, ½ cup, chopped

Cilantro, 1 cup

Directions:

1. Heat olive oil in deep cast iron skillet over medium heat.

2. Add onion and garlic and Sauté.

3. Add cumin, salt and black pepper. Sauté about 7 minutes.

4. Add corn, black beans, tomatoes, taco seasoning and cumin.

5. Let boil, cover and cook for 10 minutes.

6. Stir zucchini in. Add cheese and cook another 5 minutes.

7. Remove and top with cilantro and cumin.

8. Serve with rice.

Baked Ham
Serves: 6

Cooking time: 2 hours

Ingredients:

Picnic Ham, 4 lb

Brown Sugar, 1 cup

Water, 1 cup

Vinegar, ½ cup

Coke, 1 small

Directions:

1. Wash ham and place in cast iron skillet.

2. Combine brown sugar, water, vinegar and coke.

3. Pour over ham.

4. Cover and bake in 400F oven for 2 hours.

5. Uncover a few minutes before done so top will brown.

6. Let cool and slice.

Cast Iron Skillet Pork Chop Dinner
Serves: 4

Cooking Time: 30 minutes

Ingredients:

Oil, 2 Tbsp

Pork Chops, 4, 1-inch thick

Beef Broth, ¼ cup

Potatoes, 4 medium, cut into fourths

Carrots, 4 small, cut into chunks

Onions, 4 medium, cut into fourths

Salt, ¾ tsp

Pepper, ¼ tsp

Directions:

1. Heat oil in cast iron skillet over medium heat.

2. Cook pork chops until brown.

3. Add broth, potatoes, carrots, onions, salt and pepper.

4. Cover, reduce heat, and simmer for 30 minutes until vegetables are tender.

5. Serve with side dish of choice.

Cast Iron Skillet Southern Fried Chicken

Serves: 4

Cooking Time: 45 minutes

Ingredients:

Chicken, 1 whole, cut for frying

Buttermilk, 1 cup

Corn Meal, ½ cup

Flour, 1 ½ cup

Seasoned Salt, 2 Tbsp

Pepper, 1 Tbsp

Oil, 2 cups

Directions:

1. Soak chicken in buttermilk for 30 minutes.

2. Combine cornmeal, flour, seasoned salt and pepper.

3. Heat oil in large cast iron skillet and heat over medium heat.

4. Dip chicken in flour mixture and place in hot oil.

5. Cook for 45 minutes, turning often.

6. Remove when browned and drain.

7. Serve with sides of choice.

Cast Iron Skillet Pork Chops &Mushroom Gravy

Serves: 4

Cooking Time: 1 hour

Ingredients:

Bread Crumbs, ½ cup

Parmesan Cheese, 2 Tbsp

Pork Chops, 4

Oil, 1 Tbsp

Cream of Mushroom Soup, 1 can

Milk, ½ cup

Directions:

1. Mix bread crumbs and parmesan cheese.

2. Add pork chops and coat well.

3. Heat oil in cast iron skillet over medium heat.

4. Cook chops until browned.

5. Combine milk and mushroom soup. Add to chops.

6. Reduce heat, cover and cook for 1 hour.

7. Serve with rice or mashed potatoes.

Pork Chops With Thyme & Pineapple

Serves: 4

Cooking Time: 30 minutes

Ingredients:

Pineapple Preserves, 3 Tbsp.

Orange Juice, 3 Tbsp.

Dijon Mustard, 2 tsp

Ginger, ½ tsp

Curry Powder, ½ tsp

Pineapple Rings, 4, cut in half

Pineapple Juice, Reserved

Pork Chops, 4, thick

Butter, 2 tsp

Thyme, 2 Tbsp

Salt, ½ tsp

Pepper, ¼ tsp

Directions:

1. Mix preserves, orange juice, mustard, ginger and curry powder.

2. Heat butter in cast iron skillet over medium heat.

3. Add pork chops and season with salt, pepper and thyme.

4. Cook chops until browned. Add juice mixture.

5. Reduce heat and simmer for 30 minutes.

6. Serve with pork chop, pineapple and sauce on top.

7. Serve with side dish of choice.

Cast Iron Skillet Tuscan Pork Chops

Serves: 4

Cooking Time: 15 minutes

Ingredients:

Pork Chops, 4

Oil, 1 Tbsp

Garlic, 4 cloves, minced

Tomatoes, 1 ½ cups, diced

Onion, 1, diced

Oregano, 2 tsp

Sage, 1 tsp

Basil, 1 tsp

Directions:

1. Heat oil in cast iron skillet over medium heat.

2. Add pork chops and brown each side.

3. Add onions and reduce heat.

4. Add tomatoes, garlic, oregano, sage and basil.

5. Simmer for 15 minutes.

6. Serve over pasta.

Cast Iron Skillet Oven Baked Pork Chops

Serves: 4

Cooking Time: 45 minutes

Ingredients:

Garlic, 3 cloves, minced

Green Onion, 1, sliced

Sandwich Bread, 4 slices

Oil, 2 Tbsp

Salt, ¼ tsp

Pepper, ¼ tsp

Flour, ½ cup

Egg Whites, 3

Dijon Mustard, 3 Tbsp

Flour, 6 Tbsp

Pork Chops, 4, thick

Directions:

1. Heat oil in cast iron skillet in 350F oven.

2. Pulse bread, garlic and green onion in food processor to form crumbs.

3. Mix oil, salt and pepper. Spread crumb mixture on sheet pan and brown in oven.

4. Combine egg whites, mustard and flour.

5. Dip pork chops in egg mixture, then in bread crumb mixture.

6. Place in heated oil and bake for 45 minutes.

7. Serve with side dish of choice.

Island Pork Tenderloin
Serves: 2

Cooking Time: 30 minutes

Ingredients:

Salt, 2 tsp

Pepper, ½ tsp

Cumin, 1 tsp

Chili Powder, 1 tsp

Cinnamon, 1 tsp

Pork Tenderloins, 2

Olive Oil, 2 Tbsp

Brown Sugar, ¾ cups

Garlic, 2 Tbsp., chopped

Tabasco, 1 Tbsp

Directions:

1. Mix salt, pepper, cumin, chili powder and cinnamon.

2. Rub mixture over pork tenderloin.

3. Heat oil in large cast iron skillet, add pork and brown.

4. Combine brown sugar, garlic and Tabasco.

5. Add on top of the pork and bake in 350F oven for 30 minutes.

6. Serve with side dish of choice.

Cast Iron Skillet French Onion Pork Chops

Serves: 4

Cooking Time: 25 minutes

Ingredients:

Olive Oil, 1 Tbsp

Onions, 4 Large, sliced

Thyme, 8 sprigs

Salt, 1 tsp

Pepper, ½ tsp

Butter, 1 Tbsp

Beef Broth, ¾ cup

Red Wine, ¼ cup

Pork Chops, 4 boneless

Dijon Mustard, 4 tsp

Swiss Cheese, 4 oz., shredded

Directions:

1. Add olive oil to cast iron skillet and heat over medium heat.

2. Add onions and caramelize with thyme.

3. Add beef broth, butter, salt and pepper.

4. Simmer for 5 minutes. Remove onions.

5. Spread mustard over pork chops.

6. Place pork chops in skillet and brown on both sides.

7. Add wine, caramelized onions and pork chops.

8. Place in 350F preheated oven for 25 minutes.

9. Remove skillet and spread cheese on pork chops.

10. Return to oven and melt.

11. Remove and serve with side of choice.

Pork Chops With Brussels Sprouts And Sweet Potatoes

Serves: 4

Cooking Time: 25 minutes

Ingredients:

Mustard, 2 Tbsp

Maple Syrup, 2 Tbsp

Salt, 1 tsp

Pepper, ½ tsp

Pork Rib Chops, 4 bone-in

Canola Oil, 2 Tbsp

Brussels Sprouts, 12, trimmed and quartered

Sweet Potatoes, 2, peeled and chopped

Sage, 1 Tbsp

Directions:

1. Combine mustard and syrup.

2. Combine pepper and salt. Rub pork chop ribs with 1 tsp of mixture.

3. Heat oil in large cast iron skillet over medium heat.

4. Place Brussels sprouts and sweet potatoes in skillet. Sprinkle with rest of mixture.

5. Cook vegetables, stirring frequently. Place in bowl.

6. Add rest of oil in cast iron skillet.

7. Add pork chops and continue cooking until browned.

8. Add vegetables over pork chops.

9. Place in 350F preheated oven and cook for 25 minutes.

10. Remove and sprinkle with sage.

Cajun Spiced Pork Chops

Serves: 4

Cooking Time: 20 minutes

Ingredients:

Paprika, 1 tsp

Cumin, ½ tsp

Pepper, ½ tsp

Cayenne Pepper, ½ tsp

Sage, ½ tsp

Garlic Salt, ½ tsp

Olive Oil, 1 ½ tsp

Pork Chops, 4, center cut

Directions:

1. Combine paprika, cumin, black pepper, cayenne pepper, sage and garlic salt.

2. Rub each pork chop, coating will.

3. Heat oil in cast iron skillet over medium heat.

4. Cook pork chops for 10 minutes on each side.

5. Serve with side of choice.

Cast Iron Skillet Pork Chop Casserole

Serves: 6

Cooking Time: 55 minutes

Ingredients:

All-purpose Flour, ¾ cup

Salt, 1 tsp

Pepper, ½ tsp

Pork Loin Chops, 6

Oil, 2 Tbsp

Cream of Mushroom Soup, 1 can

Sour Cream, 1 cup

Chicken Broth, ⅔ cup

Ginger, ½ tsp

Rosemary, ¼ tsp

French-fried Onions, 1 can, divided

Directions:

1. Mix flour, salt and pepper. Coat each pork chop well.

2. Heat oil in cast iron skillet and brown pork chops.

3. Remove and add to clean cast iron skillet.

4. Combine mushroom soup, ½ cup sour cream, broth, ginger and rosemary.

5. Spread over pork chops, sprinkle half of French onions on top.

6. Cover and bake in 350F preheated oven for 50 minutes.

7. Remove and add rest of French onions. Place back in oven and cook for 5 minutes.

8. Serve with side dish of choice.

Baked Pork Chops On Rice

Serves: 4

Cooking Time: 60 minutes

Ingredients:

Cooking Spray

Pork Loin Chops, 4, boneless

White or Brown Rice, 1 cup

Cream of Celery Soup, 2 cans

Water, 2 ¼ cups

Olive Oil, 2 Tbsp

Celery, 3 ribs, sliced

Carrots, 1 can, drained

Salt, ½ tsp

Pepper, ¼ tsp

Garlic Powder, ¼ tsp

Thyme, ¼ tsp

Olive Oil, 2 tsp. for basting

Directions:

1. Mix rice, soup, water, 2 Tbsp. olive oil, celery and carrots. Pour in sprayed cast iron skillet.

2. Combine salt, pepper, garlic powder and thyme.

3. Add pork chops on top of rice.

4. Rub oil on pork chops and sprinkle with salt mixture.

5. Bake in 375F preheated oven for 60 minutes.

6. Remove when done and serve.

Cast Iron Skillet Pork Steaks

Serves: 4

Cooking Time: 30 minutes

Ingredients:

Butter, ¼ stick

Soy Sauce, ¼ cup

Green Onions, 1 bunch, sliced

Garlic, 2 cloves, minced

Pork Butt Steaks, 6

Directions:

1. Heat butter in cast iron skillet with soy sauce.

2. Sauté green onions and garlic.

3. Add pork steaks, cover and cook for 10 minutes per side.

4. Uncover and cook for 10 more minutes.

5. Serve with potatoes or green beans.

Pork Roast

Serves: 6

Cooking Time: 1 hour

Ingredients:

Pork Shoulder Roast, 3 lb

Salt, 1 tsp

Pepper, 1 tsp

Water, 1 cup

Soy Sauce, 2 Tbsp

Directions:

1. Rinse roast and place in cast iron skillet.

2. Rub with salt and pepper.

3. Combine water and soy sauce. Pour over roast.

4. Cover and cook in 350F oven for 1 hour or longer until roast is desired consistency.

5. Serve warm with side dishes of choice.

Pork Chops With Scalloped Potatoes

Serves: 6

Cooking Time: 1 hour

Ingredients:

Butter, 3 Tbsp

All-purpose flour, 3 Tbsp

Salt, 1 ½ tsp

Pepper, ¼ tsp

Chicken Broth, 1 can

Loin Chops, 6

Oil, 2 Tbsp

Potatoes, 6 peeled and sliced thinly

Onion, 1 medium, sliced

Paprika, ¼ tsp

Parsley, ¼ tsp., minced

Directions:

1. Heat oil in cast iron skillet and brown pork chops.

2. In small pan, mix butter, flour, salt, onions, pepper and broth. Heat until smooth.

3. Layer potatoes in cast iron skillet, pour flour mixture over potatoes.

4. Add pork chops and cover.

5. Bake in 350F oven for 1 hour.

6. Remove when done and sprinkle with parsley and paprika.

Cast Iron Skillet Swedish Meatballs

Serves: 4

Cooking Time: 45 minutes

Ingredients:

Oil, 2 Tbsp

Ground Beef, 2 lbs

Garlic Salt, 1 tsp.

Pepper, 1 tsp

Celery Salt, 1 tsp

Eggs, 2 beaten

Crackers, 20, crushed

Ketchup, 1 cup

Water, ½ cup

Vinegar, ⅓ cup

Brown Sugar, 4 Tbsp

Worcestershire Sauce, 2 Tbsp

Tabasco Sauce, 1 tsp

Directions:

1. Add water to crushed crackers and combine.

2. Mix ground beef, garlic salt, pepper, celery salt and eggs. Mix with cracker mixture and form into one inch balls.

3. Heat oil in cast iron skillet. Add meatballs and brown.

4. Combine ketchup, water, vinegar, brown sugar, Worcestershire sauce and Tabasco sauce.

5. Pour over meatballs and bake in 350F oven for 45 minutes.

6. Serve with mashed potatoes on the side.

Pepper Steak With Rice
Serves: 4

Cooking Time: 45 minutes

Ingredients:

Lean Beef, 1 ½ lbs. cut into strips

Paprika

Garlic, 2 cloves, crushed

Butter, 3 Tbsp

Green Onions, 1 cup, sliced

Green Peppers, 2, cut into strips

Tomatoes, 2 large, diced

Beef Broth, ¼ cup

Water, ¼ cup

Cornstarch, 2 Tbsp

Soy Sauce, 2 Tbsp

Rice, 3 cups, cooked

Directions:

1. Sprinkle steak strips with paprika. Set aside.

2. Cook steak, garlic and butter in cast iron skillet until browned.

3. Add onions and green peppers. Cook until vegetables are tender.

4. Add tomatoes and broth. Cover and simmer for 15 minutes.

5. Mix water, soy sauce and cornstarch.

6. Add to steak and cook until thickened, about 30 minutes.

7. Serve over rice.

Stuffed Cabbage Rolls

Serves: 6

Cooking Time: 40 minutes

Ingredients:

Cabbage leaves, 8 large

Tomato Soup, 1 can, divided

Ground Beef, 1 lb

Cooked Rice, 1 cup

Egg, 1 slightly beaten

Salt, 1 tsp

Pepper, 1 tsp

Directions:

1. Cook cabbage leaves in salted water a few minutes to soften.

2. Combine 2 Tbsp. of soup with ground beef, cooked rice, egg, salt and pepper.

3. Form into balls and place 1 ball in each cabbage leaf.

4. Fold sides of leaves and roll up securing with a toothpick.

5. Place rolls, seam side down in cast iron skillet.

6. Pour remaining soup over rolls and cover.

7. Cook over low heat for 40 minutes.

8. Spoon sauce over rolls while they are cooking.

9. Remove and serve.

Cast Iron Skillet Hamburger Goulash

Serves: 4

Cooking Time: 30 minutes

Ingredients:

Ground Beef, 2 lbs., cooked and drained

Salt, 1 tsp

Pepper, 1 tsp

Garlic Powder, 1 tsp

Diced Tomatoes, 1 can

Macaroni, 3 cups

Onions, ½ chopped

Green Pepper, ½ cup, chopped

Oil, 2 Tbsp

Directions:

1. Cook ground beef and drain.

2. Heat oil in skillet and Sauté onions and peppers until tender.

3. Add ground beef, tomatoes and macaroni.

4. Cook for 30 minutes until tender and macaroni is done.

5. Serve over rice.

Cast Iron Skillet Sloppy Joes
Serves: 4 to 6

Cooking Time: 30 minutes

Ingredients:

Hamburger, 1 lb

Salt, 1 tsp

Pepper, 1 tsp

Ketchup, 4 cups

Water, 2 cups

Onions, ¼ cup, chopped

Sugar, 8 Tbsp

Brown Sugar, 1 Tbsp

Worcestershire Sauce, 1 tsp

Directions:

1. Brown burger and onions in cast iron skillet and drain.

2. Add salt, pepper, ketchup, water, sugar, brown sugar and Worcestershire sauce.

3. Simmer over medium heat for 25 to 30 minutes.

4. Serve on buns with side of choice.

Cast Iron Skillet Steak Meal

Serves: 4

Cooking Time: 30 minutes

Ingredients:

Round Steak, 2 lb., cut into strips

Onion, 2 medium, sliced

Green Peppers, 2, sliced

Butter, 2 Tbsp

Cream of Celery Soup, 1 can

Water, ½ cup

Salad Dressing, ½ cup

Mushrooms, 1 can

Worcestershire Sauce, 2 Tbsp

Salt, ¼ tsp

Pepper, ¼ tsp

Directions:

1. Heat butter in cast iron skillet and brown steak strips.

2. Add onions, salt and peppers.

3. Combine soup, water, salad dressing and mushrooms.

4. Simmer for 30 minutes, adding more water if necessary.

5. Serve over noodles.

Cast Iron Skillet Meat Loaf

Serves: 4

Cooking Time: 1 hour

Ingredients:

Ground Beef, 1 ½ cup

Oatmeal, ¾ cup

Eggs, 2

Onions, ¼ cup

Salt, 2 tsp

Pepper, ¼ tsp

Ketchup, 1 cup

Brown Sugar, 2 Tbsp

Directions:

1. Combine ground beef, oatmeal, eggs, onions, salt, pepper and tomato sauce.

2. Pat into round shape and place in cast iron skillet.

3. Combine ketchup and brown sugar. Brush top of meatloaf.

4. Cook in 350F preheated oven for 1 hour.

5. Drain and slice.

6. Serve with mashed potatoes and vegetables.

Cast Iron Skillet Stroganoff

Serves: 4

Cooking Time: 30 Minutes

Ingredients:

Oil, 2 Tbsp

Sirloin Steak, 1 lb., cut into strips

Mushrooms, 1 can

Milk, ½ cup

Sour Cream, ½ cup

Salt, 1 tsp

Pepper, 1 tsp

Egg Noodles, 1 pkg. prepared

Directions:

1. Heat oil in cast iron skillet. Brown sirloin steak and mushrooms until tender.

2. Combine milk, sour cream, salt and pepper.

3. Cook noodles separately.

4. Combine steak and milk mixture, and simmer for 30 minutes.

5. Serve over noodles with hot rolls.

Cast Iron Skillet Beef Tenderloin

Serves: 4

Cooking Time: 40 minutes

Ingredients:

Beef Tenderloin, 5 lb.

Garlic Salt, 1 ¼ tsp

Red Wine, 1 cup

Soy Sauce, ¼ cup

Butter, 1 ½ sticks

Lemon Pepper, 1 tsp

Directions:

1. Grease cast iron skillet and add beef tenderloin.

2. Sprinkle with garlic salt.

3. Combine wine, soy sauce, butter and lemon pepper.

4. Pour over tenderloin.

5. Cover and bake in 425F oven for 40 minutes.

6. Serves with side dish of choice.

Cast Iron Skillet Oven Stew
Serves: 6

Cooking Time: 2 hours

Ingredients:

Lean Beef, 1 ½ lb. cut into chunks

Potatoes, 5 medium, peeled and cubed

Carrots, 2 cups, chopped

Onions, 1 cup, chopped

Celery, 1 cup, chopped

Tomatoes, 2 cans, diced

Cornstarch, 2 tsp

Sugar, 1 tsp

Pepper, 1 tsp

Salt, 1 tsp

Directions:

1. Place beef chunks in large cast iron skillet.

2. Add potatoes, carrots, onions, celery, tomatoes, sugar, cornstarch, pepper and salt.

3. Cover skillet and cook at 350F for 2 hours or until meat and vegetables are tender.

4. Serve with bread.

Cast Iron Skillet Salmon Loaf

Serves: 4

Cooking Time: 1 hour

Ingredients:

Salmon, 1 lb., boneless

Bread Crumbs, ½ cup

Pepper, ¼ tsp

Salt, ½ tsp

Parsley, 1 tsp

Egg Yolks, 2

Lemon Juice, 1 Tbsp

Milk, ½ cup, hot

Butter, 2 Tbsp., melted

Celery, ½ cup, chopped

Egg Whites, 2, beaten

Directions:

1. Combine Salmon, bread crumbs, pepper, salt, parsley, egg yolks, lemon juice, milk, butter and celery. Fold in beaten egg whites.

2. Form into round loaf and place in cast iron skillet.

3. Cover and bake for 1 hour in 350F oven.

4. Serve with dill sauce on the side.

Garlic Shrimp
Serves: 6

Cooking time: 25 minutes

Ingredients:

Fresh Shrimp, 2 dozen

Olive Oil, ¼ cup

Parsley, ¼ cup, chopped

Garlic, 3 cloves, minced

Red Pepper, ½ tsp., dried

Pepper, ¼ tsp

Butter, ¼ stick

Breadcrumbs, ½ cup

Parmesan Cheese, ½ cup

Directions:

1. Peel and devein shrimp.

2. Place shrimp in large cast iron skillet.

3. Pour oil over shrimp.

4. Combine parsley, red pepper, pepper and garlic.

5. Sprinkle mixture over shrimp.

6. Cover and bake at 300F for 15 minutes.

7. Turn shrimp, drizzle with butter, breadcrumbs and parmesan cheese.

8. Bake uncovered for 10 more minutes.

9. Serve warm.

Cast Iron Skillet Fried Cat Fish
Serves: 4

Cooking Time: 30 minutes

Ingredients:

Catfish Fillets, 1 lb

Flour, 1 cup

Corn Meal, ½ cup

Salt, 1 tsp

Pepper, ½ tsp

Buttermilk, 1 cup

Oil, 1 cup

Directions:

1. Combine flour, cornmeal, salt and pepper.

2. Heat oil in cast iron skillet over medium heat.

3. Dip catfish fillets in buttermilk, then in flour mixture.

4. Drop into hot oil and cook for 30 minutes or less, turning while cooking for even browning.

5. Drain on paper towel.

6. Serve with hush puppies and coleslaw.

Cast Iron Skillet Flounder

Serves: 6

Cooking Time: 20 minutes

Ingredients:

Lemon Juice, ½ cup

Worcestershire Sauce, ¼ cup

Dry White Wine, 1 ½ cup

All-purpose Flour, 2 cups, sifted

Pepper, ¼ tsp

Salt, ¼ tsp

Paprika, ¼ tsp

Eggs, 6

Parsley, ½ cup, chopped

Flounder, 8

Butter, ½ stick

Lemon wedge for garnish

Directions:

1. Combine wine, lemon juice and Worcestershire sauce and set aside.

2. Mix flour, pepper, salt and paprika together.

3. Whisk eggs and parsley.

4. Place flounder in wine mixture for 2 minutes.

5. Dip flounder in flour mixture.

6. Dip flounder in egg and parsley mixture.

7. Melt butter in cast iron skillet over medium heat.

8. Cook in heated butter for 10 minutes on each side.

9. Turn while cooking to keep from burning.

10. Garnish with lemon wedges.

Salmon Patties

Serves: 4

Cooking Time: 25 minutes

Ingredients:

Salmon, 1 can, boneless

Onions, ¼ cup diced

Egg, 1

Saltine Crackers, 4 crushed

Pepper, ½ tsp

Salt, 1 tsp

Cornmeal, 1 ½ cup

Oil, 1 cup

Directions:

1. Heat oil in cast iron skillet over medium heat.

2. Combine salmon, onions, egg, crackers, salt, pepper and cornmeal.

3. Form into patties and fry in heated oil for 20 to 25 minutes, turning continuously.

4. Drain on paper towel.

5. Serve with side dishes of choice.

Crab Roll-ups
Serves: 4

Cooking Time: 30 minutes

Ingredients:

Cooking Spray

Italian Tomato Sauce, 1 can

Crab Flakes, 1 pkg.

Cottage Cheese, 1 cup, drained

Parmesan Cheese, ¼ cup

Egg, 1

Parsley Flakes, 1 tsp.

Onion Powder, ¼ tsp

Lasagna Noodles, 6

Directions:

1. Cook noodles ahead of time.

2. Combine tomato sauce, crab flakes, cottage cheese, egg, parsley flakes and onion powder. Mix well.

3. Spoon mixture on each lasagna noodles and roll up.

4. Place seam down in sprayed cast iron skillet.

5. Bake in 375F preheated oven for 30 minutes.

6. Remove and garnish with cheese.

Polish Sausage And Sauerkraut
Serves: 4

Cooking Time: 1 hour, 40 minutes

Ingredients:

Bavarian Style Sauerkraut, 2 jars

Brown Sugar, 1 ½ cups

Bacon, ½ lb

Polish Sausage, 2 ½ lb

Directions:

1. Drain and rinse kraut.

2. Cook and drain bacon. Mix kraut, bacon, water and brown sugar.

3. Simmer in cast iron skillet for 1 hour.

4. Cook polish sausage for 20 minutes and cut into 1 inch pieces.

5. Combine sausage and kraut mixture and cook for 20 minutes.

6. Serve warm.

Corn Casserole With Smoked Sausage

Serves: 4

Cooking Time: 50 minutes

Ingredients:

Smoked Sausage, 1 pkg., cut into 1 inch pieces

Cream Corn, 2 cans

Cheddar Cheese, 2 cup

Green Chiles, 1 cup, drained

Onion, ½ cup, chopped

Milk, 1 cup

Eggs, 2 large

Cornmeal, 1 cup

Garlic Salt, 1 tsp.

Baking Soda, ½ tsp

Directions:

1. Combine cream corn, cheese, green chilies, onion, milk and eggs.

2. Mix cornmeal, garlic salt and baking soda.

3. Combine corn mixture with cornmeal mixture. Add cut smoked sausage.

4. Pour into sprayed cast iron skillet and bake at 350F for 50 minutes.

5. Casserole is done when fork comes out clean.

Potato and Smoked Sausage Skillet
Serves: 4

Cooking Time: 30 minutes

Ingredients:

Potatoes, 3, peeled and sliced

Onions, ½, sliced

Salt, ½ tsp

Pepper, ½ tsp

Oil, 2 Tbsp

Directions:

1. Heat oil in cast iron skillet over medium heat.

2. Add sliced potatoes and onions.

3. Salt and pepper. Cook for 20 minutes until potatoes are tender.

4. Add smoked sausage and cook for 10 more minutes.

5. Serve warm.

Lamb Chops

Serves: 4 to 6

Cooking Time: 25 minutes

Ingredients:

Soy Sauce, ¼ cup

Honey, ¼ cup

Tarragon Vinegar, ¼ cup

Lamb Chops, 4

Tomato, 4 slices

Garlic Salt, ¼ tsp.

Directions:

1. Combine soy sauce, honey and vinegar.

2. Place chops in mixture and marinade.

3. Arrange lamb chops in cast iron skillet. Brush with some of the marinade.

4. Bake in 350F oven for 25 minutes until done.

5. Top lamb chops with tomatoes and sprinkle with garlic salt.

6. Serve with a nice side salad and roll.

Venison Chops

Serves: 8

Cooking Time: 30 minutes

Ingredients:

Venison Chops, 8

Boiled Ham, 8 slices

Butter, 1 stick

Onions, 2 medium, chopped fine

Mushrooms, 12, sliced

Parsley, 2 Tbsp., minced

Salt, ½ tsp

Pepper, ½ tsp

Sour Cream, 8 Tbsp

Heavy Aluminum Foil, 8 sheets

Directions:

1. Melt half of the butter in large cast iron skillet. Sauté the chops for 10 minutes.

2. Remove and keep warm. Melt the remaining butter.

3. Sauté onions, mushrooms and parsley. Add salt and pepper.

4. Prepare foil packet with ham slice, venison chop, and 2 Tbsp. of onion mixture.

5. Add a Tbsp. of sour cream and seal.

6. Bake in 350F preheated oven for 20 minutes.

7. One pack serving per person.

8. Serve with baked beans and coleslaw.

BOOK 4

CAST IRON SKILLET COOKBOOK: VOL.4 DESSERT AND SIDE DISH RECIPES

Introduction

Its dessert time and the cast iron skillet is the perfect skillet for the job. The baking is phenomenal in a cast iron skillet. Cake, pies and cobblers are delicious. So get your skillet out and oil it for that delectable dessert.

The cast iron skillet you use for desserts should never be used for cooking meats and savory meals. Your cast iron skillet can take on the flavors of whatever you are cooking. I'm sure you would not want your cake tasting like steak. You can salt scrub your skillet if you only have one skillet. It should also be oiled and used only for baking or for the dessert of your choice. If possible get two skillets, one for meats and one for desserts.

As with other cast iron dishes, the desserts prepared will also be wonderful. The heat is evenly conducted with cast iron, so baking is a perfect skillet to use as a baking dish.

The cast iron skillet creates homey and comfort desserts. The desserts are easy to make and are not time consuming. Desserts are the perfect thing for beginners to cook in cast iron, but they are also perfect for the novice. A little flour, sugar, milk and fruit can end in a delicious cobbler or tart. Cakes cook wonderful in cast iron. The contained heat evens out the cooking process for a cake. Your cakes will come out beautifully browned and delectable. Always preheat your skillet whether baking or cooking on top of the stove. It creates even cooking.

Cast iron cooking is an art. The older recipes have been handed down for generations. But do not fret; new ones are on the way. You are the creator of these delectable recipes. You can also take the older recipes and add or take from the original to make something new. Our parents and grandparents were not on fast food. As a matter of fact, there were not any fast food places available as there is today.

Many hours were spent in the kitchen preparing meals. Eating out was a treat done on holidays or trips. Spend a little more time in your kitchen cooking with your cast iron skillet. Do not be afraid to experiment with your choice of ingredients. Your cast iron skillet awaits you.

Home-style desserts can be symbolized by no other cookware like cast iron. It has been handed down for generations and once again is growing in popularity. It was the original non-stick skillet before Teflon. There are drawbacks of rust and pitting with cast iron skillets. Be sure and oil often to keep them from rusting and to fill in the pits. If your skillet is taken care of properly, it will serve you well, as well as whomever you pass it on to.

Use your cast iron skillet for more than meats and cornbread. Begin making cobblers, pies, cakes and tarts. The ideas are endless. It will go from stovetop to oven with ease. Believe it or not cookies and dessert bars are wonderful cooked in cast iron. The middle to the edge cooks evenly.

There is always room for desserts, especially if you have a family with a sweet tooth. It is the final course to a wonderful meal. It seems there is always room for dessert. Some families have gotten away from have a full meal with dessert, but now it can be brought back.

While the family is enjoying the meal, dessert can be cooking in your cast iron skillet in the oven. There is nothing like warm cobbler with ice cream and coffee after the meal. This can bring back family time at the kitchen table.

The cast iron skillet is wonderful for many of your side dishes. The seasoned skillet makes vegetables taste delectable. It adds the finishing touch to a meal of roast or meatloaf.

With so many side dish recipes, the cast iron skillet will withstand the heat of your oven or stovetop. A campfire works wonders too. There are wonderful fried potato recipes, as well as garden vegetable recipes. Breads can be made in your cast iron skillet. Prepare a yeast bread or good cornbread to go along with the great vegetables.

The wonderful thing about cast iron skillets is that it can be used for much of what is cooked in your kitchen. Breakfast, lunch, dinner and desserts can be prepared in this skillet. Make sure to add a skillet to your kitchen collection and begin creating the wonderful recipes handed down to you or created by you. You will not regret the addition to your culinary collection.

When you purchase your skillet, season it and store properly. Make it a trusted part of your kitchen. You will love it and your family will love you for all the tasty treasures coming out of your skillet!

DESSERTS & SIDE DISHES

Broccoli Casserole

Serves: 6

Cooking Time: 30 minutes

Ingredients:

Broccoli, 2 pkg., frozen and chopped

Margarine, 1 stick

Mushroom Soup, 1 can

Cheese, ¾ lb

Ritz Crackers, 1 sleeve, crushed

Directions:

1. Cook broccoli as directed on package.

2. Drain and put in large cast iron skillet.

3. Melt margarine, soup and cheese.

4. Pour over broccoli.

5. Sprinkle crackers on top.

6. Bake in preheated oven for 30 minutes until brown and bubbly.

Cowboy Beans

Serves: 6 to 8

Cooking Time: 60 minutes

Ingredients:

Pork and Beans, 1 can drained

Hamburger, 1 lb., cooked

Onion, 1 cup chopped

Brown Sugar, ½ cup

Molasses, ¼ cup

Ketchup, ¼ cup

Mustard, 1 Tbsp

Barbecue Sauce, ½ cup

Salt, ¼ tsp

Pepper, ¼ tsp

Directions:

1. Brown hamburger and onion together and drain.

2. Stir in other ingredients, place in cast iron skillet.

3. Bake in 350F preheated oven for 1 hour.

4. Remove and serve with meal.

Fried Cabbage

Serves: 4

Cooking Time: 30 minutes

Ingredients:

Cabbage, 3 cups finely chopped

Butter, 2 Tbsp

Onion Powder, ½ tsp

Caraway Seeds, ¾ tsp

Salt, ½ tsp

Pepper, ½ tsp

Oil, 1 Tbsp

Directions:

1. Heat oil in cast iron skillet over medium heat.

2. Add butter and melt.

3. Add cabbage, onion powder, caraway seeds, salt and pepper.

4. Cover and cook for 30 minutes. Stir often.

5. Remove and serve with main meal.

Cheesy Scalloped Potatoes

Serves: 4

Cooking Time: 1 hour

Ingredients:

Cheese, 1 cup, shredded

Mushroom soup, 1 can

Milk, ⅔ cup

Pepper, 1 tsp

Salt, 1 tsp

Potatoes, 4 cups, sliced thin

Onion, 1, sliced thin

Butter, 1 Tbsp

Paprika, ¼ tsp

Directions:

1 Combine soup, butter, milk, salt and pepper.

2. Layer potatoes, onions, cheese and soup mixture in cast iron skillet.

3. Cover and bake at 375F for 1 hour.

4. Remove from oven and let sit to settle.

5. Serve warm.

Potato Cakes
Serves: 4 to 6

Cooking Time: 15 minutes

Ingredients:

Mashed Potatoes, 3 cups, leftover

Seasoned Salt, 1 Tbsp

Pepper, 1 Tbsp

Oil, ½ cup

Flour, ¼ cup

Directions:

1. Heat oil in cast iron skillet over medium heat.

2. Combine potatoes, salt, pepper and flour.

3. Form into patties and place in heated oil.

4. Brown on each side for a total of 15 minutes each.

5. Drain on paper towel and serve warm.

6. These are wonderful with meatloaf and vegetables.

Fried Green Tomatoes
Serves: 4

Cooking Time: 5 minutes

Ingredients:

Cornmeal, ⅔ cup

Salt, ¼ tsp

Pepper, ¼ tsp

Green Tomatoes, 3 large, sliced

Egg, 1

Oil, ½ cup

Directions:

1. Heat oil in cast iron skillet over medium heat.

2. Combine cornmeal, salt and pepper and set aside.

3. Beat egg.

4. Dip tomatoes slices in eggs, then in cornmeal mixture.

5. Add to hot oil and fry for 5 minutes or until browned, turning once.

6. Drain on paper towel and serve.

Baked Macaroni And Cheese
Serves: 4 to 6

Cooking Time: 20 minutes

Ingredients:

Cheddar Cheese Soup, 1 can

Milk, ½ cup

Pepper, ¼ tsp

Salt, ¼ tsp

Butter, 2 tsp., melted

Bread Crumbs, 4 Tbsp.

Macaroni, 2 cups, cooked

Directions:

1. Combine soup, milk, salt and pepper.

2. Stir in cooked macaroni.

3. In separate bowl combine butter and bread crumbs.

4. Add macaroni mixture to greased cast iron skillet.

5. Sprinkle bread crumbs on top.

6. Bake in 400F preheated oven for 20 minutes.

7. Serve warm.

Corn Pudding

Serves: 4

Cooking Time: 50 minutes

Ingredients:

Eggs, 4

Milk, 4 cups

Corn, 2 cups, whole kernel

Cream Style Corn, 1 can

Flour, 7 Tbsp., all-purpose

Sugar, ½ cup

Salt, 1 ½ tsp

Butter, 2 sticks, melted

Directions:

1. Grease cast iron skillet.

2. Combine all ingredients.

3. Pour into cast iron skillet.

4. Bake at 350F for 50 minutes.

5. Serve warm.

Scalloped Green Peppers

Serves: 4

Cooking Time: 30 minutes

Ingredients:

Diced peppers, 1 ½ cup, cooked about 5 minutes

Cracker Crumbs, 1 ½ cup

Butter, 1 stick

Cheddar Cheese, 1 ½ cup, grated

Red Pepper, ¼ tsp

Salt, ½ tsp

Milk, 1 ½ cup

Directions:

1. Sauté cracker crumbs in butter.

2. Grease cast iron skillet.

3. Layer peppers, cheese and seasonings in cast iron skillet.

4. Pour milk over layers.

5. Bake covered in 350F preheated oven for 10 minutes.

6. Remove cover and sprinkle bread crumbs over top.

7. Bake for 20 minutes or until slightly brown.

Green Bean Casserole

Serves: 4

Cooking Time: 30 minutes

Ingredients:

Cream of Mushroom Soup, 1 can

Milk, ½ cup

Soy Sauce, 1 tsp

Pepper, ¼ tsp

Green Beans, 4 cups, cut and cooked

Fried Onions, 1 ⅓ cup

Directions:

1. Preheat oven to 325F.

2. Combine soup, milk, soy sauce, pepper, beans, and ⅔ cup of fried onions.

3. Pour into cast iron skillet.

4. Bake for 25 minutes or until hot.

5. Remove and sprinkle rest of fried onions on top.

6. Bake an additional 5 minutes.

7. Remove from oven and serve warm.

Rice Casserole

Serves: 4

Cooking Time: 1 hour

Ingredients:

Long Grain Rice, 1 cup, uncooked

Beef Consommé, 1 can

Onion Soup, 1 can

Mushrooms, 8 oz. can

Directions:

1. Preheat oven to 350F.

2. Combine all of the ingredients.

3. Bake for 1 hour.

4. Serve warm.

Maple-Glazed Carrots

Serves: 4

Cooking Time: 45 minutes

Ingredients:

Carrots, 6 medium, cut into ¼ inch slices

Maple Syrup, 2 Tbsp

Butter, 1 Tbsp

Cinnamon, 1 tsp

Nutmeg, ¼ tsp

Salt, ¼ tsp

Pepper, ¼ tsp

Directions:

1. Steam carrots until tender.

2. Combine maple syrup, butter, cinnamon and nutmeg in cast iron skillet until butter is melted.

3. Add carrots and cook over medium heat, stirring occasionally, until carrots are glazed.

4. Season with salt and pepper prior to serving.

Cast Iron Skillet Mexican Cornbread
Serves: 6

Cooking Time: 45 minutes

Ingredients:

Oil, ¼ cup

Corn Meal, 2 cups, self-rising

Jalapeno Peppers, ¼ cup, diced

Whole Kernel Corn, 1 can

Milk, 1 cup

Egg, 1

Directions:

1. Preheat oven to 350F.

2. Add oil to cast iron skillet and place in oven to heat.

3. Combine corn meal, peppers, corn, milk and egg.

4. Remove hot skillet and add corn bread mixture.

5. Bake for 45 minutes or until bread is golden brown and done in the middle.

6. Serve as side to main meat dish.

Fried Okra
Serves: 6

Cooking Time: 20 minutes

Ingredients:

Okra, 2 lbs., sliced

Corn Meal, ¾ cup

All-purpose flour, ½ cup

Salt, ½ tsp

Vegetable Oil, ¼ cup

Directions:

1. Heat oil in cast iron skillet over medium heat.

2. Combine okra, corn meal, flour and salt. Coat okra well.

3. Place okra in heated oil.

4. Brown on both sides. Stir. About 5 minutes.

5. Place in preheated 350F oven for 10 minutes.

6. Remove and serve warm.

Roasted Vegetables

Serves: 6

Cooking Time: 15 minutes

Ingredients:

Cooking Spray

Broccoli Florets, 2 cups

Mushrooms, 2 cups

Butternut Squash, 2 cups, chopped

Zucchini, 1, sliced and quartered

Yellow Squash, 1, sliced and quartered

Red Bell Pepper, 1, chopped

Red Onion, 1, chopped

Olive Oil, 2 Tbsp

Balsamic Vinegar, 2 Tbsp

Garlic, 2 cloves, minced

Thyme, 1 ½ tsp

Salt, ¼ tsp

Pepper, ¼ tsp

Directions:

1. Spray cast iron skillet with cooking spray.

2. Combine broccoli, mushrooms, butternut squash, zucchini, yellow squash, bell pepper and onion. Place in cast iron skillet.

3. Add vinegar, garlic and thyme.

4. Sprinkle with salt and pepper. Toss and coat.

5. Bake in 425F preheated oven for 15 minutes until tender.

6. Serve warm.

Caramelized Brussels Sprouts

Serves: 4

Cooking Time: 20 minutes

Ingredients:

Olive Oil, 2 Tbsp

Brussels Sprouts, 3 cups, sliced in half

Onion, 1, chopped

Sesame Seeds, 2 Tbsp

Salt, ½ tsp

Directions:

1. Toast sesame seeds in cast iron skillet for 6 minutes. Remove and set aside.

2. Heat oil in cast iron skillet over medium heat. Add onions and caramelize. Remove and set aside.

3. Heat the remaining oil in skillet and add Brussels sprouts. Cook for 7 minutes on one side. Turn and cook the other side for 7 minutes, caramelizing both.

4. Combine onions with Brussels sprouts.

5. Remove and sprinkle with sesame seeds and salt.

6. Serve warm.

Fried Squash Patties

Serves: 4

Cooking Time: 10 minutes

Ingredients:

Oil, ½ cup

Squash, 3 cups, grated

Baking Mix, ⅔ cup

Cheese, ½ cup, shredded

Onion, ⅓ cup, chopped

Egg, 1

Directions:

1. Combine all ingredients.

2. Heat oil in cast iron skillet over medium heat.

3. Drop a spoonful at a time in hot oil and flatten.

4. Brown on both sides. Approximately 5 minutes per side.

5. Drain on paper towel.

6. Salt and serve warm.

Asparagus And Onions

Serves: 4

Cooking Time: 30 minutes

Ingredients:

Olive Oil, ¼ cup

Asparagus, 1 bunch, cleaned

Red Onion, 1 sliced long ways

Brown Sugar, 2 Tbsp

Directions:

1. Heat oil in cast iron skillet.

2. Add onion and brown sugar. Cook until onions are caramelized.

3. Add asparagus and simmer for 15 to 20 minutes.

4. Remove and serve warm.

Cornbread Stuffing
Serves: 6

Cooking Time: 30 minutes

Ingredients:

Cornbread, 1 skillet cooked

Cornbread Stuffing Mix, 1 box

Butter, ½ stick

Onion, 1 small, diced

Celery, 3 stalks, diced

Sage, ¼ cup

Cream of Chicken Soup, 1 can

Chicken Broth, 2 cans

Salt, 1 tsp

Pepper, 1 tsp

Directions:

1. Sauté onions and celery in butter in cast iron skillet over medium heat.

2. Combine cornbread, stuffing mix and spice, sage, cream of chicken soup, celery, onions, sage, chicken broth, salt and pepper. Pour into cast iron skillet.

3. Cook in 350F oven for 30 minutes or until hot.

4. Serve with chicken or turkey.

Onion Rings
Serves: 2

Cooking Time: 20 minutes

Ingredients:

Vidalia Onion, 1 large, sliced and onion rings separated

Oil, 1 cup

Flour, 2 cups

Cornmeal, ½ cup

Seasoned Salt, 2 tsp

Pepper, 1 tsp

Garlic Powder, ½ tsp

Onion Powder, ½ tsp

Eggs, 2

Milk, 1 cup

Directions:

1. Heat oil in cast iron skillet over medium heat.

2. Combine flour, cornmeal, seasoned salt, pepper, garlic powder and onion powder in deep bowl.

3. Mix eggs and milk well

4. Dip each onion ring in egg mixture, then dredge in flour mixture.

5. Drop into hot oil. Brown on each side about 10 minutes.

6. Drain on paper towel.

7. Great with burgers or any sandwich.

Onion Pie

Serves: 6

Cooking Time: 40 minutes

Ingredients:

Bermuda Onions, 2 ½ lbs., peeled and sliced

Butter, 4 Tbsp

Salt, 1 tsp

Cheddar Cheese, 1 cup

Flour, 2 Tbsp

Eggs, 2

Pepper, 1 tsp

Worcestershire Sauce, 1 tsp

Tabasco Sauce, ½ tsp

Sour Cream, ¼ cup

Pastry, enough for 1 pie crust

Directions:

1. Heat butter in cast iron skillet over medium heat. Add onions and sauté.

2. Add salt and cheese and heat.

3. Remove skillet and let cool.

4. Add flour, egg, pepper, Worcestershire sauce and Tabasco.

5. Stir in sour cream and heat.

6. Press pastry in cast iron skillet. Fill with mixture.

7. Cook for 30 to 40 minutes until crust is light brown.

8. Cool before serving.

Creamed Spinach

Serves: 4

Cooking Time: 15 minutes

Ingredients:

Onion, 1 small, minced

Garlic, 2 cloves, crushed

Butter, 2 Tbsp

Flour, 1 Tbsp

Frozen Spinach, 1 pkg., cooked and drained

Salt, ¼ tsp

Sour Cream, 1 cup

Bacon, 3 slices, cooked and crumbled

Directions:

1. Sauté onions and garlic in butter in cast iron skillet.

2. Add flour and cook for 1 to 2 minutes.

3. Add spinach and salt. Cook for 10 to 13 minutes.

4. Remove and add sour cream and top with bacon.

5. Serve warm.

Fried Corn
Serves: 2

Cooking Time: 20 to 30 minutes

Ingredients:

Corn, 2 cans, drained

Oil, 1 Tbsp

Salt, 1 tsp

Pepper, 1 tsp

Directions:

1. Heat oil in cast iron skillet over medium heat.

2. Add corn, salt and pepper.

3. Cook until browned.

4. Serve with any main dish.

5. Super easy recipe.

Fried Squash

Serves: 4

Cooking Time: 20 minutes

Ingredients:

Yellow Squash, 3 small, cleaned and sliced

Oil, ½ cup

Cornmeal, 1 cup

Flour, ¼ cup

Seasoned Salt, 2 tsp

Pepper, 1 tsp

Garlic Powder, 1 tsp

Egg, 1

Milk, ½ cup

Directions:

1. Heat oil in cast iron skillet over medium heat.

2. Combine cornmeal, flour, salt, pepper and garlic powder in deep bowl.

3. Beat egg and milk together.

4. Dip squash slices in egg mixture, then in cornmeal mixture.

5. Place in hot oil and cook for approximately 10 minutes on each side or until done.

6. Makes an excellent vegetable side dish.

Cast Iron Skillet Cauliflower

Serves: 6

Cooking Time: 20 minutes

Ingredients:

Cauliflower, 1 head, washed and separated into florets

Eggs, 2, beaten well

Water, ¼ cup

Salt, ½ tsp

Pepper, ¼ tsp

Flour, ½ cup

Dry Bread Crumbs, 1 cup

Oil, 1 cup

Directions:

1. Preheat oil in cast iron skillet over medium heat.

2. Combine eggs, water, salt and pepper.

3. Mix flour and dried breadcrumbs together

4. Dip cauliflower in flour mixture, dip in egg mixture, then re-dip in flour mixture.

5. Drop in hot oil and cook for 20 minutes, turning to get even brownness.

6. Drain on paper towel and serve.

Cast Iron Skillet Asparagus

Serves: 6

Cooking Time: 20 minutes

Ingredients:

Asparagus, 2 lbs, ends cut off and cleaned

Water, 1 cup

Salt, 1 tsp

Hollandaise Sauce, 1 jar

Directions:

1. Heat water in cast iron skillet over high heat.

2. Add asparagus and salt.

3. Bring to boil, cover and cook for 20 minutes or until tender.

4. Remove and drain.

5. Place in dish and pour Hollandaise sauce.

6. Serve warm.

Cast Iron Skillet Carrot Cake

Serves: 10

Cooking Time: 40 minutes

Ingredients:

Sugar, 2 cups

Oil, 1 ½ cups

Eggs, 4, beaten

Self-Rising Flour, 2 cups

Cinnamon, 2 tsp

Vanilla Extract, 2 tsp

Carrots, 3 cups, grated

Nuts, ½ cup, chopped

Butter, ½ stick

Cream Cheese, 1 pkg.

Confectioners' Sugar, 1 lb. box

Milk, if needed

Directions:

1. Oil cast iron skillet well and place in 300F oven.

2. Combine sugar, oil, eggs, flour, cinnamon, 1 tsp. of vanilla, carrots and nuts.

3. Pour into the cast iron skillet and bake for 40 minutes or until fork pulls out clean.

4. Cream butter, cream cheese and confectioner's sugar. Add milk if needed to achieve consistency.

5. Spread icing on cool cake.

6. Slice and serve.

Caramel Nut Pound Cake

Serves: 8

Cooking Time: 1 hour

Ingredients:

Butter, 2 sticks

Shortening, ¼ cup

Brown Sugar, 1 lb. box

Sugar, 1 cup

Eggs, 5

Cake Flour, 3 cups

Salt, ½ tsp.

Baking Powder, 1 tsp.

Vanilla Extract, 1 Tbsp

Milk, 1 cup

Walnuts, 1 cup, chopped finely

Directions:

1. Grease large cast iron skillet and place in 325F preheated oven.

2. Cream butter and shortening until smooth.

3. Add brown sugar and sugar. Mix. Add eggs one at a time and mix.

4. Sift flour, salt, and baking powder.

5. Combine flour mixture and brown sugar mixture. Add milk and vanilla and blend well.

6. Add nuts and combine.

7. Pour in heated cast iron skillet and cook for 1 hour.

8. Serve warm or cool.

Heath Bar Cake

Serves: 6

Cooking Time: 45 minutes

Ingredients:

Oil, ¼ cup

Flour, 2 cups

Vanilla Extract, 1 Tbsp

Sugar, 1 cup

Milk, 1 cup

Baking Cocoa, ¼ cup

Caramel Ice Cream Topping, 1 jar

Cool Whip, 1 container

Heath Bars, 1 pkg., crushed

Directions:

1. Grease cast iron skillet and heat in 350F preheated oven.

2. Combine flour, vanilla extract, sugar, milk and cocoa. Mix well.

3. Pour into preheated skillet.

4. Cook for 45 minutes or until the center is done.

5. Remove and pour caramel ice cream topping on cake.

6. Let cool and spread with cool whip.

7. Top with crushed Heath Bars. Slice and serve.

Cast Iron Skillet Honey Bun Cake

Serves: 6

Cooking Time: 40 minutes

Ingredients:

Yellow Cake Mix, 1 box

Oil, ⅔ cup

Sour Cream, 8 oz.

Eggs, 4

Cinnamon, 1 Tbsp

Brown Sugar, 1 cup

Powdered Sugar, 2 ½ cup

Milk, ½ cup

Vanilla, 1 tsp

Directions:

1. Mix cake mix, oil, sour cream and eggs. Combine well.

2. Pour ½ batter into greased cast iron skillet.

3. Mix cinnamon and brown sugar. Sprinkle over batter.

4. Pour remaining batter over the cinnamon and brown sugar.

5. Bake for 40 minutes in 350F oven.

6. While cake is baking, mix powdered sugar, milk and vanilla.

7. Remove cake when done, poke holes in cake and pour powdered sugar mixture over top of cake.

8. Slice and serve.

Fudge Cake
Serves: 6

Cooking Time: 45 minutes

Ingredients:

Brown Sugar, 1 ½ cup

Butter, 1 stick

Shortening, ½ cup

Eggs, 2

Salt, ½ tsp

Baking Powder, 1 tsp

Vanilla, 2 tsp.

Flour, 2 ¼ cup

Milk, 1 cup

Cocoa, ½ cup

Hot Water, ⅓ cup

Directions:

1. Pour water over cocoa.

2. Cream sugar and shortening and add eggs.

3. Sift flour and baking powder together and add cream mixture and cocoa.

4. Add vanilla, combine and pour into greased cast iron skillet.

5. Bake for 45 minutes at 350F. Serve warm.

Crumb Cake

Serves: 6 to 8

Cooking Time: 45 minutes

Ingredients:

Oil, 1 tsp

Flour, 2 ½ cups

Salt, ¼ tsp

Brown Sugar, 1 cup

Butter, ½ stick

Baking Powder, 1 tbsp

Milk, ¾ cup

Vanilla, 1 tsp

Baking Soda, 2 tsp

Directions:

1. Mix flour, salt, brown sugar, butter and baking powder.

2. Set aside 1 cup of mixture for crumb topping.

3. Add milk, vanilla and baking soda to other crumb mixture.

4. Pour into greased cast iron skillet and bake for 45 minutes in 350F oven.

5. When done, remove and sprinkle with crumb topping.

Brownie Pudding Cake

Serves: 6

Cooking Time: 45 minutes

Ingredients:

Flour, 1 cup

Baking Powder, 2 tsp

Salt, ½ tsp

Sugar, ¾ cup

Cocoa, 2 Tbsp. plus ¼ cup

Milk, ½ cup

Vanilla, 1 tsp

Oil, 2 Tbsp

Brown Sugar, ¾ cup

Directions:

1. Combine flour, baking powder, salt, sugar, 2 Tbsp. cocoa, milk, vanilla and oil.

2. Pour into greased cast iron skillet.

3. Combine brown sugar and ¼ cup of cocoa.

4. Sprinkle over top of flour mixture.

5. Bake in 350F oven for 45 minutes.

6. Serve warm.

Chocolate Cobbler Cake

Serves: 6

Cooking Time: 45 minutes

Ingredients:

Butter, 1 stick

Flour, 1 cup

Sugar, 1¾ cup

Milk, ½ cup

Cocoa, 6 Tbsp

Boiling Water, 1 ½ cup

Pecans, ½ cup

Directions:

1. Preheat oven to 350F.

2. Melt butter in cast iron skillet.

3. Combine flour, ¾ cup sugar, milk, pecans and 2 Tbsp. cocoa.

4. Pour into melted butter.

5. Combine cocoa and sugar and spread over the first mixture.

6. Pour the boiling water over all.

7. Bake for 45 minutes.

8. Serve warm with whipped topping.

Blackberry Betty

Serves: 6

Cooking Time: 45 minutes

Ingredients:

Blackberries, 1 qt.

Lemon Juice, 1 Tbsp.

Cinnamon, ¼ tsp.

Flour, 1 cup

Sugar, 1 cup

Butter, 1 stick

Directions:

1. Preheat oven to 375F.

2. Place berries in large cast iron skillet.

3. Sprinkle with lemon juice and cinnamon.

4. Combine flour, sugar and butter until crumbly.

5. Sprinkle over berries and bake for minutes.

6. Serve with whipped cream.

Apple Pie

Serves: 6

Cooking Time: 35 minutes

Ingredients:

Pie Crust, 1 pkg. of two

Sugar, 1 cup, plus 1 Tbsp

Butter, ½ stick

Flour, ¼ cup

Water, 2 Tbsp

Apples, 8 cups, peeled, cored and sliced

Cinnamon, 1 ½ tsp

Nutmeg, 1 tsp

Allspice, ½ tsp

Salt, ½ tsp

Directions:

1. Preheat oven to 425F.

2. Combine 1 cup sugar and butter in cast iron skillet until mixture bubbles.

3. Add flour and blend.

4. Add water and apples and cook over low heat until apples are tender.

5. Add cinnamon, nutmeg, allspice and sauce.

6. Place pie crust in bottom of cast iron skillet and bring up the sides.

7. Pour mixture into pie crust, add other pie crust on top and bake 35 minutes or until golden brown.

8. Serve with ice cream on the side.

Cast Iron Skillet Pecan Pie

Serves: 6

Cooking Time: 45 minutes

Ingredients:

Eggs, 3 slightly beaten

Dark Corn Syrup, 1 cup

Sugar, 1 cup

Salt, ¼ tsp

Butter, 2 Tbsp

Vanilla, 1 tsp

Pecans, 1 cup, whole

Pie Crust, 1 pkg.

Directions:

1. Preheat oven to 400F.

2. Place pie crust in cast iron skillet, making sure to go up the sides.

3. Combine all ingredients and pour into skillet.

4. Bake 15 minutes, lower heat to 350F, then bake 30 more minutes.

5. Remove and let cool.

6. Slice and serve.

Lazy Fruit Cobbler

Serves: 4 to 6

Cooking Time: 1 hour

Ingredients:

Butter, 1 stick

Self-rising flour, 1 cup

Sugar, 1 cup

Milk, ¾ cup

Sweetened Fruit, 1 qt. of your choice

Vanilla, 1 tsp

Directions:

1. Preheat oven to 350F.

2. Melt butter in cast iron skillet.

3. Mix flour, sugar, milk and vanilla. Combine well and pour over butter.

4. Pour sweetened fruit over the flour mixture in the middle of the skillet.

5. Bake for 1 hour.

6. Remove and let sit.

7. Serve warm or cool with ice cream on the side.

Cast Iron Skillet Peanut Butter Cookie

Serves: 4 to 6

Cooking Time: 15 minutes

Ingredients:

All-purpose Flour, 1 ½ cup

Baking Powder, 1 ½ tsp

Salt, ½ tsp

Vegetable Oil, ⅔ cup

Creamy Peanut Butter, ½ cup

Brown Sugar, 1 cup

Egg, 1

Vanilla Extract, ½ tsp

Cooking Spray

Directions:

1. Combine flour, baking powder and salt.

2. Blend oil with peanut butter.

3. Gradually add brown sugar, creaming until light and fluffy.

4. Add egg and vanilla, beat well.

5. Blend in flour mix and mix well.

6. Spray cast iron skillet with cooking spray.

7. Spread mixture in skillet.

8. Bake for 15 minutes or until golden brown.

9. Remove, cool and cut as pie slices.

Cast Iron Skillet Blondies

Serves: 4

Cooking Time: 25 minutes

Ingredients:

Self-rising Flour, 1 ½ cup

Butter, 1 stick, melted

Brown Sugar, 2 cups

Vanilla, 1 tsp

Eggs, 2

Directions:

1. Preheat oven to 350F.

2. Mix all ingredients and pour into well-oiled cast iron skillet.

3. Bake for 25 minutes or until a toothpick inserted in the middle comes out clean.

4. Cool before serving.

Magic Cookie Bars

Serves: 4 to 6

Cooking Time: 30 minutes

Ingredients:

Butter, 1 stick

Graham Cracker Crumbs, 1 ½ cups

Sweetened Condensed Milk, 1 can

Semi-sweet Chocolate Chips, 1 6-oz pkg.

Butterscotch Chips, 1 6-oz. pkg.

Coconut, 1 cup

Chopped Nuts, 1 cup

Directions:

1. Preheat oven to 350F.

2. Melt butter in cast iron skillet.

3. Sprinkle graham cracker crumbs in melted butter.

4. Sprinkle milk, chocolate chips, butterscotch chips, coconut and chopped nuts.

5. Press down in skillet.

6. Bake for 30 minutes.

7. Remove, let cool, the cut in squares or slices.

Oatmeal Cookie Patties
Serves: 6 to 8

Cooking Time: 20 minutes

Ingredients:

Butter, 2 cups

Sugar, 2 cups

Brown Sugar, 2 cups

Eggs, 4

Vanilla, 2 tsp

Quick-cooking Oats, 2 cups

Corn Flakes, 2 cups

All-purpose Flour, 4 cups

Baking Powder, 2 tsp

Baking Soda, 2 tsp

Semi-Sweet Chocolate Chips, 1 pkg.

Pecans, 2 cups, chopped

Directions:

1. Cream butter, sugar and brown sugar until smooth.

2. Add eggs 1 at a time, mixing well after each egg.

3. Stir in vanilla, oats and corn flakes.

4. Sift flour, baking powder and baking soda together. Gradually add to creamed mixture.

5. Add chocolate chips and pecans. Pour into cast iron skillet.

6. Bake in 325F oven for 20 minutes.

7. Cool and serve.

No-Crust Coconut Pie

Serves: 8

Cooking Time: 1 hour

Ingredients:

Eggs, 4

Butter, ½ stick

Sugar, 1 cup

Flour, ¼ cup

Baking Powder, ½ tsp

Milk, 2 cups

Vanilla, 1 tsp

Salt, ¼ tsp

Coconut, 1 cup

Directions:

1. Combine eggs, butter, sugar, flour, baking powder, milk, vanilla, salt and coconut. Blend until smooth.

2. Pour into oiled cast iron skillet.

3. Bake at 350F for 1 hour.

4. Crust will form as it cooks.

Blueberry Bread

Serves: 9

Cooking Time: 40 minutes

Ingredients:

Flour, 2 cups

Sugar, ¼ cup

Baking Soda, ½ tsp

Salt, ½ tsp

Molasses, ¼ cup

Yogurt, 1 cup

Butter, 2 Tbsp., melted

Egg, 1 beaten

Blueberries, 1 cup

Directions:

1. Combine flour, sugar, baking soda and salt.

2. Combine molasses, yogurt, butter and eggs. Mix well

3. Stir in dry ingredients. Fold in blueberries.

4. Pour into oiled cast iron skillet.

5. Bake at 350F for 40 minutes.

Cast Iron Skillet Strawberry Peach Tart

Serves: 6

Cooking Time: 35 minutes

Ingredients:

Peaches, 2, fresh, peeled, pitted and sliced

Strawberries, 2 cups

Sugar, 2 Tbsp

Vanilla Extract, 1 tsp

Pie Crust, 1 pkg., prepared

Egg, 1 beaten

Directions:

1. Preheat oven to 425F.

2. Combine peaches and strawberries with sugar and vanilla. Coat well.

3. Unfold crust and line cast iron skillet with crust hanging over the skillet.

4. Spoon fruit into center of crust. Fold edges over the fruit.

5. Pour some of the juice over the fruit.

6. Brush crust with egg and sprinkle with sugar.

7. Bake for 35 minutes or until golden brown.

8. Serve warm.

Cast Iron Skillet Berry Dessert

Serves: 8

Cooking Time: 45 minutes

Ingredients:

Mixed Berries, 2 lbs

Sugar, ¼ cup plus 2 Tbsp

Water, 2 Tbsp

Lemon Juice, 1 Tbsp

Self-rising Flour, 1 cup

Salt, ¼ tsp

Buttermilk, ½ cup plus 2 Tbsp

Butter, 2 Tbsp., melted

Cinnamon Sugar, 1 ¼ tsp

Directions:

1. Cook berries, water, lemon juice, and ¼ cup of sugar in cast iron skillet over medium heat until thick. About 15 minutes.

2. Mix flour, salt and sugar. Add buttermilk and butter. Mix until moist dough appears.

3. Drop by spoonfuls on top of berry mixture.

4. Sprinkle with cinnamon sugar.

5. Cook for about 30 minutes until dumplings set.

Cast Iron Skillet Monkey Bread

Serves: 4 to 6

Cooking Time: 30 minutes

Ingredients:

Sugar, ½ cup

Cinnamon, 1 Tbsp

Butter, 1//2 cup

Brown Sugar, 1 cup

Frozen Dinner Rolls, 1 pkg.

Cream Cheese, 1 pkg. cut into cubes

Pecans, 1 ½ cup, chopped

Directions:

1. Combine sugar and cinnamon.

2. Place a cube of cream cheese into the center of each roll.

3. Roll the stuffed roll in the sugar mixture.

4. Place rolls in cast iron skillet.

5. Melt butter and add brown sugar. Combine well.

6. Pour mixture over rolls.

7. Bake at 350F for 30 minutes.

8. Gooey goodness!

Cast Iron Skillet Strawberry Shortcake

Serves: 6

Cooking Time: 35 minutes

Ingredients:

Crust:

Cake Flour, 1 cup

Sugar, 3 Tbsp.

Butter, ⅓ cup, softened

Filling:

Sugar, 1 ¼ cup

Butter, 1 ½ stick

Egg, 1

Flour, 1 cup

Evaporated Milk, ⅔ cup

Light Corn Syrup, ¼ cup

Vanilla, 1 tsp

Powdered Sugar, for dusting

Topping:

Strawberries, 1 lb., quartered

Heavy Whipping Cream, 2 cups

Directions:

1. Prepare crust and press into bottom of cast iron skillet.

2. Preheat oven to 350F.

3. Cream together sugar, butter, egg, flour milk, corn syrup and vanilla. Mix well.

4. Pour filling into skillet with crust and sprinkle with powdered sugar.

5. Bake for 35 minutes.

6. Whisk whipping cream.

7. Pour strawberries into center of cake and top with whipped cream.

8. Serve each slice with whip cream.

Salted Caramel Apple Crumble
Serves: 6

Cooking Time: 30 minutes

Ingredients:

Sugar, 1 ⅓ cups

Water, ¼ cup

Salt, 1 ¼ tsp

Heavy Cream, ¾ cup

Butter, 9 Tbsp

Vanilla, 1 tsp

All-purpose Flour, 1 cup

Brown Sugar, ⅓ cup

Apples, 4 granny smith, peeled, cored and sliced

Lemon Juice, 2 Tbsp

Directions:

1. Make caramel sauce first by heating sugar and water over medium heat. Add in salt and cream. Cook until smooth. Stir in butter and vanilla.

2. Combine flour, brown sugar, sugar, butter and ½ tsp. salt. Mix until crumbly.

3. Toss apples in lemon juice and cook in cast iron skillet over medium heat.

4. Pour caramel sauce into apples and stir. Top with crumble.

5. Bake in 350F oven for 30 minutes. Serve with caramel sauce sprinkled over the mixture.

Cast Iron Skillet Smores

Serves: 2

Cooking Time: 10 minutes

Ingredients:

Chocolate Chips, 1 cup

Marshmallows, 8 large

Graham Crackers, 1 pkg. for dipping

Directions:

1. Heat oven to 450F.

2. Pour chocolate chips into cast iron skillet.

3. Top with large marshmallows.

4. Bake for about 10 minutes or until marshmallows are browned.

5. Remove and serve with graham crackers.

Blueberry & Cream Cheese Croissant Pudding

Serves: 6

Cooking Time: 45 minutes

Ingredients:

Croissants, 4, sliced and dried

Cream Cheese, 1 pkg

Blueberries, 1-16 oz. can in syrup

Cream, 2 ½ cups

Eggs, 6

Sugar, 1 cup

Vanilla Extract, 1 Tbsp

Directions:

1. Combine cream, eggs, sugar and vanilla. Blend well and set aside.

2. Press ⅓ of each croissant in bottom of cast iron skillet.

3. Layer with cream cheese and blueberries.

4. Top with other half of croissant and press down.

5. Bake in oven at 350F for 45 minutes.

6. Serve warm.

Banana Nut Bread

Serves: 6

Cooking Time: 35 minutes

Ingredients:

Bananas, over-ripe, 3

Eggs, 2

All-purpose Flour, 2 cups

Allspice, ¼ tsp

Baking Soda, 1 tsp

Brown Sugar, ½ cup

Sugar, ½ cup

Mace, ground, ¼ tsp

Salt, ½ tsp

Vanilla, 1 tsp

Pecans, 1 cup

Butter, 1 ½ stick

Buttermilk, ⅓ cup

Directions:

1. Heat cast iron skillet in 350F preheated oven.

2. Mash bananas, add buttermilk, butter, vanilla and eggs. Mix well.

3. Mix flour, allspice, baking soda, brown sugar, mace, pecans and salt.

4. Combine wet and dry mixtures.

5. Pour into cast iron skillet greased with butter.

6. Bake for 35 minutes or until done in middle.

English Toffee

Serves: 8

Cooking Time: 15 minutes

Ingredients:

Butter, 1 cup

Sugar, 1 ¼ cups

Water, 2 Tbsp

Almonds, ¼ cup

Chocolate Chips, 1 cup

Directions:

1. Melt butter in cast iron skillet over medium heat.

2. Add sugar and water and bring to boil.

3. Add almonds. Sprinkle chocolate chips on top.

4. Let stand 1 minute, spread chocolate over the top.

5. Let cool and break into pieces.

Cast Iron Skillet Crepes

Serves: 4

Cooking Time: 60 seconds per crepe

Ingredients:

Flour, 1 cup

Sugar, 1 Tbsp.

Salt, ¼ tsp.

Milk, 1 ⅓ cup

Vanilla, 1 Tbsp.

Eggs, 3

Butter, 3 Tbsp.

Sugar, for sprinkling

Directions:

1. Combine flour and salt.

2. Combine milk, vanilla, eggs and butter.

3. Pour in milk and egg mixture into flour mixture.

4. Preheat cast iron skillet coated with butter over medium heat.

5. Pour ¼ cup of mixture into hot skillet and brown on each side for 30 seconds until golden brown.

6. Sprinkle with sugar and roll up.

7. Serve warm.

Cast Iron Skillet Giant Chocolate Chip Cookie
Serves: 8

Cooking Time: 40 minutes

Ingredients:

Flour, 2 cups

Baking Soda, 1 tsp

Salt, ½ tsp

Butter, ¾ cup, softened

Sugar, ½ cup

Brown Sugar, ¾ cup

Egg, 1

Vanilla, 1 Tbsp.

Milk, 1 Tbsp.

Chocolate Chips, 1 bag

Directions:

1. Heat oven to 350F.

2. Combine flour, baking soda and salt.

3. Mix butter and sugars. Cream together.

4. Add egg, vanilla and cream. Mix well.

5. Combine flour mixture and cream mixture.

6. Add chocolate chips.

7. Press into cast iron skillet.

8. Bake about 40 minutes until edges are browned.

Printed in Great Britain
by Amazon